Rethink

REACH
THEM ALL

with

Learning Stations

HOW TO CREATE AND USE LEARNING STATIONS TO GET GROWTH OUT OF EVERY STUDENT

FOR K-12 MATH TEACHERS

Chris Skierski

Reach Them All

—

Use Learning Stations to Reach Every Student

Author: Chris Skierski

Cover Design: Chris Skierski

Photos and Illustrations: Chris Skierski

Wellington, Florida

Text Copyright © Chris Skierski. 2018

Illustrations Copyright © Chris Skierski. 2018

Photos Copyright © Chris Skierski. 2018

ISBN: 978-1723146671

ISBN: 1723146676

Rethink Math Teacher

www.rethinkmathteacer.com

Table Contents

Introduction

What do you do when you teach something in your math class, but many of your students don't get it? And many of those who don't get it, don't get it for different reasons?

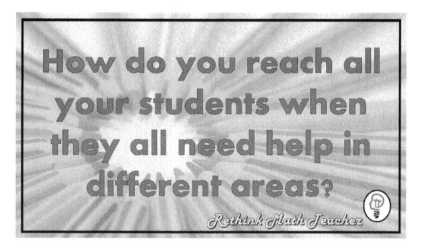

Many math concepts involve a series of steps to solve the problem correctly. For example, think of the steps involved in solving a long division problem:

STEP 1	STEP 2
$$12\overline{)432} \\ \ 36$$ with quotient 3	$$12\overline{)432} \\ -36 \\ \ \ \ 7$$ with quotient 3
STEP 3	STEP 4
$$12\overline{)432} \\ -36\,| \\ \ \ 72$$ with quotient 3	$$12\overline{)432} \\ -36 \\ \ \ 72 \\ -72$$ with quotient 36

Step one involves multiplication. Step two is subtracting double-digit numbers. Step three has to do with the long division process and an understanding of place values. Step four, again is multiplication, but also includes tracking, which again involves understanding the long division process.

Or consider what's involved in solving a two-step equation:

$$-3x + (-2) = -17$$

Adding Integers $+2 \qquad +2$

$$-3x = -15$$

Solve One-Step Equations

Divide Integers $\div(-3) \quad \div(-3)$

$$x = 5$$

When you teach these or other math skills that have multiple steps in the process, you will have students who can't complete the problem, but for different reasons. Some will struggle with the first step, others with the second, and so on.

How do you reach all your students when they all need help in different areas?

In the pages that follow, I will share with you how I wrestled with this question. There were many strategies that I was using as a teacher that I thought were effective. However, as I considered these methods in light of the goal of reaching all of my students, I realized that these strategies were not in the best interest of everyone in the room.

In the end, I learned that I could reach each and every one of my students, regardless of what they needed work on, or what was holding them back, by differentiating instruction with learning stations. My strongest students could move ahead, at whatever pace suited them, while my weakest students received all the practice and time that they needed. Even my chronically absent students were no longer left behind, but continued to grow and be challenged in the appropriate areas.

Learning stations allowed me to reach every student in my class in a meaningful and impactful way. This success was evident on the state diagnostics as my class had learning gains that were close to 100%. This methodology also helped my students feel successful and reduced behavioral issues. These successes were not missed by my administrators, who rapidly promoted me.

You too can have the same impact on your students, and together we will walk through how this process can help you reach them all.

Chapter 1 — From Fired to Assistant Principal

Have you ever felt the frustration of knowing that you weren't reaching most of your students and that they weren't growing the way you expected? Have you ever felt like an ineffective teacher?

I was at my second school in three years and looked out on a room full of disinterested, floundering students who'd lost the belief that I could help them grow.

The weaker students had been left behind as I pushed the class through the majority of the curriculum. They didn't understand most of what we had covered, so they sat in the room pretending to try or misbehaving. The bad grades that they received no longer affected them, as they had lost hope and saw no signs of relief.

Yet the stronger students had been held back as I tried to reteach the class the material that the majority of them had not mastered. They too sat in my class, bored of having to re-practice skills that they had already learned; yearning to be challenged, wanting to be pushed on to more difficult tasks.

 Overall, there was very little growth.

I became frustrated with them, and they with me. Soon their complaints to their parents trickled to the ears of my administrators, who felt the same way I did – that I was not affecting growth in my students – that I had failed to reach them all.

NEW BEGINNINGS – HAPPY ENDINGS

I didn't finish the year at that school. I was removed from the class due to my ineffectiveness and was asked not to return. In my newfound free time, I began to pay closer attention to the keys of being an effective teacher. I read a lot on classroom management, I rededicated myself to emphasizing relationships and being positive, and I really started to pay attention to strategies that had a positive impact on student growth.

That fall I began teaching at my third school in four years. But this time I felt more confident in many of the things that I had learned and was prepared to impact all of my students.

By the end of that first year at this school, my students' had remarkable test scores, and I would be promoted to the head of the math department. The next year, I began to develop learning stations in my classroom, which helped my classes reach almost 100% learning gains on the state assessments, and I was promoted to administration. After three years, I was named the Assistant Principal and now serve on the Coalition of Math Teachers in my district.

I was asked not to return to the school I was working at. Three years later I was an Assistant Principal

Rethink Math Teacher

That's quite a change in three short years. But before we focus on the principles that I learned to be an effective teacher, I think it's important to focus on the journey. So, allow me to take you back to that painful year where I realized that I was not having an impact on my students; a realization shared by my administrators. Let me take you back to that place where I learned five valuable lessons – five mistakes that I was making as a math teacher that were destroying my effectiveness.

Section 1 – I was Doing it All Wrong

Chapter 2 - Five Mistakes I was Making as a Math Teacher

After not being allowed to finish the year in the classroom, I began to reflect upon some of the reasons that caused me to be an ineffective teacher.

I realized that I was making several mistakes that were preventing my students from growing. If I was going to be an effective teacher, and reach all of my students, I had to correct these errors so that my students could grow.

How Great am I?

Early in the year, my Geometry classes had to learn the midpoint formula.

If you're not familiar with this formula, it's used to find the midpoint of two points on a coordinate plane. To get the solution, you have to add the values of both points (their x values and their y values) and then divide them by two. A fairly easy skill for Geometry students.

Midpoint Formula

$$x = \frac{x_1 + x_2}{2}, \; y = \frac{y_1 + y_2}{2}$$

I noticed that when one of the point's coordinates had a negative value, many of the students were getting the wrong answer. It quickly became apparent that they could not add integers (positive and negative numbers).

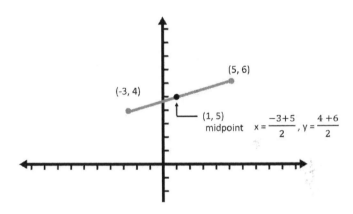

In the example above, the left coordinate's x value is negative three. To find the x value of the midpoint, we add negative three and five (the x value of the right coordinate) and divide by two. Making the midpoint's x value equal one. But many of my students were getting this wrong because they did not know the answer to negative three plus five. They couldn't add integers!

Not worried, I got a class set of integer chips (also called counter chips) and spent an entire day reteaching the class how to add integers and modeling this with counter chips. My students worked out several problems using the manipulatives to re-discover the skill and were given plenty of practice.

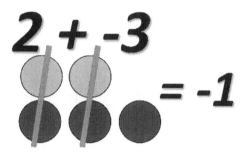

The next day, we resumed work on the midpoint formula. But to my shock, there was no noticeable improvement! The majority of the class, despite my excellent reteach lesson the previous day, still could not add integers!

Frustrated with their lack of progress, even though I had retaught the skill, I pushed them through the remainder of the section – which most of them did not do well on because they lacked the prerequisite skill of adding integers which is needed to complete the task at hand.

As I reflected on this, and many similar incidents, I realized that the majority of the students in my class had experienced no growth despite all the time we had spent on that unit.

The weaker students finished the section still not knowing how to add integers, so they couldn't complete the midpoint formula, nor could they perform any of the other skills that followed due to a lack of prerequisite skills that I had not effectively retaught them.

The stronger students did not need to spend all that extra time on the skill, they already knew how to add integers and had mastered the midpoint formula. They were ready to move on to higher level skills, but I prevented them from doing so by forcing them to participate in all the reteaches.

Ironically, the weaker students had been left behind, and the stronger students were held back.

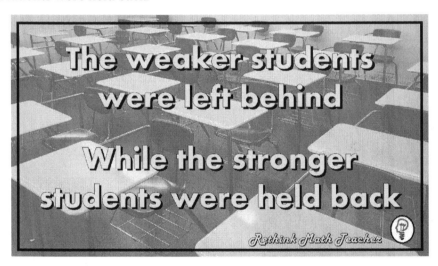

A Painful Reflection

When I went through my education courses, I was taught to reflect upon the effectiveness of each lesson. This time, however, I began to reflect upon the effectiveness of me as a teacher – and the methods I was using.

I began to consider how students learn and realized that I was doing several things as an educator that were stifling my students' growth.

What follows is a list of 5 mistakes I was making as a Math Teacher

1) I was leaving students behind

The first, and what may be the biggest mistake that I was making as a math teacher is that I was constantly leaving students behind. I would teach a concept, give what I felt was a sufficient amount of practice, then give them a test, and then move on to the next skill.

For example, I would teach adding integers, give a day or two of practice, and then move on to subtracting integers. However, to subtract integers, you have to be able to add integers. So all of my students who had not grasped adding integers had no chance of mastering subtracting integers. Yet I was forcing them to move on to this skill, even though I knew that they couldn't do the work.

I realized that many math concepts build upon each other.

How could a student multiply double digit numbers, if they don't know their times tables? How could they add fractions with uncommon denominators, if they can't convert fractions? How can they graph a line, if they don't understand slope?

Yet as a teacher, I was ignoring my weaker students, dragging them through the material, knowing that they couldn't comprehend it because they lacked the prerequisite skills.

What message was I sending to the student that I was forcing to move on to more difficult concepts though they weren't ready? What was I saying to them, when after failing the test, I progressed them to the next standard?

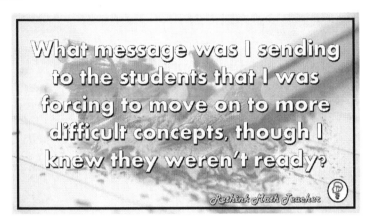

If I was going to be an effective teacher, and reach all of my students, I had to start expecting mastery. And if I truly wanted to impact all of my students, I couldn't ignore some of them simply because they weren't learning at the same pace as the majority of the class.

This meant that if a student didn't pass the test with a sufficient score, I couldn't move them on to the next standard, I had to retain them on that skill until they were proficient at it.

2) I was holding my best students back

As mentioned in the section above, when I was focusing on giving the whole class a reteach, though some didn't need it, I was holding my stronger students back from reaching their truest potential.

Two years after the story I mentioned in chapter one, I was teaching an intensive math class at a Title 1 school. (Intensive math is a class for students who are below grade level. Title 1 schools are schools that have a large percentage of students from economically disadvantaged homes). Though all the students in the class started below grade level, I had 10% of my students test in the top 10% of students in the state at the end of the year. This was on account of me allowing them to move on to more advanced skills, though the majority of the class wasn't ready to move on with them.

Reaching all of your students means not ignoring the stronger ones, but challenging them and pushing them further ahead.

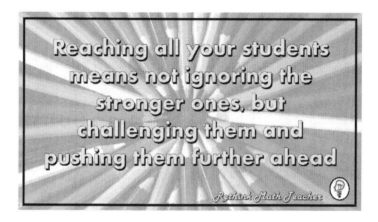

3) I was penalizing failure

Different people learn different skills at different paces.

There are some skills that I am a fast learner at; snowboarding and surfing are not those skills. It took me way more practice than the average person to become proficient at both of these skills.

For some people, the skill that takes them longer to learn is math. This doesn't make them dumb, or a failure, it just means that they need more time and more practice than most.

But the way that I was teaching did not accommodate such students. I forced them through the curriculum at a pace that they couldn't handle, all the while labeling them as a failure because they needed more practice, or because they started off knowing less than the rest of the class.

Failure is a great teacher. It helps us understand what doesn't work, and why. It also forces us to reevaluate our methods, searching for the reason it was incorrect. Such evaluation causes reflection, and eventually, correction.

I knew all of this to be true. Yet as a math teacher, I was penalizing my students for failing by giving them bad grades, and then not giving them the opportunity to feel success because I didn't give them another opportunity on the task that they had failed.

What if I had a snowboarding teacher who pulled me through snowboarding classes the way I was pulling my students through math class? I would have been trying to go down black diamonds or land complicated jumps when I still couldn't stop. I also would have grown to hate the sport and wanted to quit. I would have despised my teacher, and worst of all, I never would have felt the joy of being successful.

If failure is part of the learning process, why was I punishing my students for it?

I realized that if I wanted to reach my students, I had to help them fail effectively - to learn from their mistakes, without fearing them, or being punished for making them. I had to help students get up after failing and try again so that they could eventually grow.

4) I was not celebrating success

I was teaching a middle school math class, and I was allowing one of my students to work on a skill until she passed it. She was a very low leveled math student who always tested in the bottom quartile of students in the state. She hated math and had learned very little of it by the time she entered my sixth-grade math class.

The first time she tested on the skill we were working on, she failed it. She was used to getting F's on her math tests, so it didn't bother her too much. I encouraged her to try again, and let her know that when she passed the test, she would earn an A and it would replace the F.

The next attempt on the test was not much better, but I encouraged her to keep trying and spent extra time trying to help her be successful. On her third attempt, she scored a D, which I put in the grade book, replacing the previous F score.

It took some time, but eventually, she mastered the skill and got an A on the test. When I handed it to her, she cried. She told me, through sobs and tears, that she had never gotten an A before, and that she couldn't wait to show her parents. (We actually called them together on my planning period. That was a really cool moment).

If learning is such an important thing, why wasn't I celebrating it with my students when it happened?

5) I was reinforcing bad habits

I don't golf, but I am told that it is harder to unlearn a bad habit, then it is to learn a good habit. So, if someone holds the golf club wrong, and practices that way over and over again, it will be hard to break this routine and teach them the right way to hold the golf club.

You've probably noticed something similar with the way some of your students hold a pencil when they write.

I realized that I was giving students practice problems to do, but I wasn't giving them immediate feedback. Thus, they were often making the same mistake over and over again, on multiple problems, without ever learning from their mistakes. In a sense, I was reinforcing a bad habit by not correcting their mistakes.

If I wanted my students to grow, I had to give them immediate feedback when they are learning a new skill.

These five mistakes were hurting my effectiveness and hindering my students' growth.

1) I was leaving students behind

2) I was holding my best students back

3) I was penalizing failure

4) I was not celebrating success

5) I was reinforcing bad habits

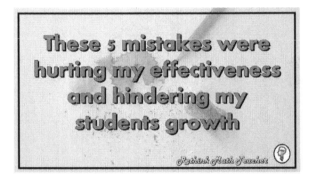

If I wanted to be an effective teacher, I needed to figure out how to deliver instruction, without repeating these errors.

Chapter 3 – Breaking the Mold

One year for Christmas, a student's mom gifted me a large ham. Excited, I brought it home to my recently married wife, who shared my enthusiasm. Then she cut the ends off and put it in the pan to cook. Shocked, I asked why she cut the ends off. My wife informed me that this is how you cook a ham. To which I responded, "Why?"

My wife admitted that she didn't know why you needed to cut the ends off of a ham to cook it, but that's how her mother taught her to cook one. So we called her mother, who also did not know why you cut the ends off of a ham to cook it. But she added that that was the way that her mother taught her.

So my wife and her mother called my wife's grandmother and asked her why you need to cut the ends off of a ham to cook it. Her grandmother responded, "Well I don't know why you two are doing it, but I always had to cut the ends off so that it would fit in my roasting pan."

The Teacher Mold

As I considered the mistakes that I was making as a teacher, I realized that the majority of them revolved around my instructional delivery method.

I was teaching my classes the same way I had been taught; probably the same way that my teachers were taught, most likely the same way that teachers have been delivering instruction for decades.

My class period looked like this: I taught the skill, modeled a few problems to the class, and then gave them the opportunity to practice independently before going over the correct way to solve those problems in front of the class. We did several problems like this before moving onto some form of independent practice that would be graded for accuracy.

This form of instructional delivery does not reach all the students in the room. Instead, it treats them like an assembly line. Students are lumped together based on their age, not their ability, and education is delivered to them in a one-size-fits-all methodology. Those who do not pace with the rest of the class are labeled as problematic, and discarded (left behind).

If I was going to reach all my students, and help each one grow, this delivery system had to change. I realized that whole group instruction was not ideal, it was merely convenient.

This became apparent when I was teaching two-step equations to my students. As the students were doing their independent practice, I circulated the room, helping students with their work. Most of the students were stuck, and couldn't get the correct answer. But each

21

student was stuck for a different reason. Several students could not add integers, several others couldn't subtract them, and others couldn't multiply and divide integers. There were also some students who couldn't complete a one-step equation.

As I worked with these students, I was hit with an epiphany: If a student had not mastered one of the prerequisite skills, they couldn't complete the grade level work.

The students who struggled with adding integers would never be able to solve a one or two-step equation until they first mastered adding integers. I could show videos, use manipulatives, and model the correct format, trying to teach them two-step equations until I was blue in the face... if they couldn't add integers, they couldn't complete a two-step equation.

But how could I serve those students, without making the whole class review adding integers, thus stifling their growth? What about those who could add integers, but couldn't subtract? What about those who could do both of those, but didn't know how to multiply and divide integers? How could I reach all of them? How could I make all of them rise, so that they could all do the grade level work?

I decided that I needed to develop a system where those who needed help on the first skill got specific, targeted help on that skill; while those needing help on the second skill were equally supported, and all the way down the line of various prerequisite skills.

I started looking at the math work, not as an assembly line where students were forced through the same processes at the same pace, but as a ladder, where students mastered one skill and then progressed to the next, ultimately climbing to the top.

I envisioned a room where all twenty (plus) students were each getting targeted help on the skill that they needed to work on. As they mastered that one skill, they moved to the next, gaining confidence as they progressed.

The focus was no longer on exposing the class to the entire curriculum without them learning most of it, but on mastering as many skills as each student could, so that each student experienced success and growth.

I also began to look at other teaching common practices that may not be in the best interest of learning...

Chapter 4 - Teaching Against the Grain

Five Common Teaching Practices that I Abandoned

Penalizing Failure, Not Expecting Mastery

As I began developing a method to reach each student where they needed help and having them master a skill before moving on to the next one; I began to ponder something I heard Sal Khan of Khan Academy say in a Ted Talks presentation.

"The traditional (teaching) model penalizes you for experimentation and failure, but it does not expect mastery.[1]"

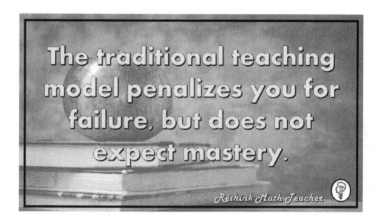

If you had read that quote to me before I started this journey, I would have said, "That statement did not apply to me! Of course I expect my students to master what I am teaching!"

But the truth is that I did not expect my students to master the skills I taught, because when they didn't master something, I gave them a bad grade and we all moved on to the next skill.

This left those students who hadn't mastered the previous standard ill-prepared to master the next concept. There was no remediation, no reteach, no sending them back to that skill to work on it until they truly 'got it;' I just pushed them on to the next section. Which they inevitably failed – since usually, the skills build upon each other.

Not only was I not expecting them to master the skill, I was punishing them for their failures.

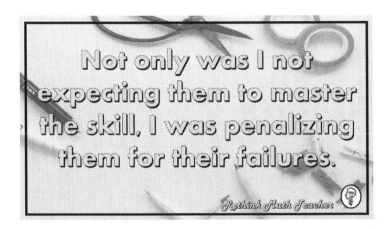

Not only was I not expecting them to master the skill, I was penalizing them for their failures.

Rethink Math Teacher

We all know that we learn through failures. Mistakes and errors are great teachers, both in life and in academia. Yet, in my classroom – and in many classrooms – when you fail, you get a bad grade, and then we move on. There's no learning from the mistakes. No encouragement to make new and better mistakes. No wrestling with the subject matter, nor productive struggle. Just drill and repeat. Here's how to do it, now you do it this way over and over again until it's memorized.

But how could I not penalize a student for making mistakes, while still holding him accountable to learn the material? How could I encourage experimentation, while still expecting mastery?

How could I not penalize them for making mistakes,
while still holding them accountable?

I began to reflect upon how one learns a new skill, like surfing, welding, the proper form for a golf swing, or multiplying fractions.

First, the correct way is modeled, then you practice, and then you learn from your successes or failures. And if you want to master the skill, you continue to practice until you master it.

Like Learning to Ride a Bike

Imagine this scenario:

I'm trying to teach a child to ride a bike. So I begin by having her practice with training wheels. I explain and model how to ride a bike, and then give her some practice on the bike.

Then, after three days of this teaching and practice, I give her a test. But the test revealed that this young child still could not balance well, constantly fell down on left turns (despite the training wheels), and had not mastered the skill of coming to a complete stop!

So I label her with a D, remove the training wheels, and begin teaching her how to ride a bike!

This would not make sense! Of course I would reteach her, try to help her correct these mistakes, and help her master each skill before progressing her to riding a bike with no training wheels! Because without these skills that I was trying to teach her with the training wheels, she will not be successful at riding a bike without them!

Sadly, this is how I was treating my math students. I taught them a skill, they learned it or they didn't, and we moved on!

So I decided that I was going to give my students the ability to stay on a skill as long as they needed, without penalizing them for their slower-than-average pace. If one student took an extra week or more on the first skill, I resolved that this was okay. The value was in mastering that skill so that they could master the next. Of course I would give them extra help, and work my best so that they weren't stuck on one skill for too long. But I was going to encourage them to take as long as they needed, and their grade would not be impacted by their pace.

But they won't get through the entire curriculum in one year

I decided that most of my students did not master the entire curriculum from the previous year.

I also decided that there was more value in my students mastering a few skills, then in seeing all the skills but mastering none of them.

I get a lot of pushback on this idea. I am amazed at how many of us in the teaching world feel that there is more value in our students seeing every chapter of the textbook than there is in those students mastering any of them.

Getting through the entire curriculum was no longer a priority, growth was. If my students learned one standard last year, and I was able to get them to fully master four or five, I felt that they had been successful, even if they never saw the last chapter in the textbook.

Getting through the entire curriculum was no longer a priority, growth was.

Celebrate Success

Earlier, I told you about a student who worked on a skill for a long time, finally mastered it, and earned an A. She was so proud of herself, and I was too. I bet she went home and showed that paper to her parents. She probably even put it on the fridge in the kitchen. And I know that her success on that day helped motivate her to work harder on the next skill she faced in our math class.

Success should be celebrated.

When people are successful in other areas of life, they get trophies, certificates, plaques, and people make a big deal about it... shouldn't it be the same way with academics? Honestly, what's more important than a child's education?

So I decided that we would make milestones out of student success.

You finally mastered how to simplify fractions! Your name's going on the wall! And I'm giving you a certificate of achievement to take home to your parents... who, by the way, I'm calling to share the good news!

Everyone loves to be successful, and they love to be celebrated.

In fact, I'm willing to bet that a lot of the discipline issues that we see in our classrooms are from kids who have been left behind, and don't think that they will ever have a chance of being successful in school. So they have given up and checked out.

But what if that student knew that you weren't giving up on him? And that you had given him work that was exactly where he needed it. And that he could work on it for as long as he needed, and when he finally mastered it, he would get to truly feel accomplished?

That student might be willing to work harder for you than he otherwise would have. And when he finally tastes success, he'll want more, and he'll be armed with the confidence that he needs to press on.

Practice Makes Permanent

The great Vince Lombardi is famously credited for saying:

Practice does not make perfect, it makes permanent. Perfect practice makes perfect.

I have coached a lot of basketball. One of the great frustrations I have is getting a student in middle or high school, who has a terribly ugly shot: two hands on the ball, shooting from the chest, the ball has side spin on, the list goes on. It's so painful to try and un-teach him this improper way, and then reteach him the proper way. It takes hundreds, if not thousands, of repetitions for progress to be made, which is such a battle in this 'results now' culture that we live in. It would have been so much easier if he had just been taught the right way from the beginning.

The same thing is happening with our students in math class. They are working on a skill, like adding fractions but they are doing it incorrectly by adding the denominators instead of converting to the common denominator. Yet, no one catches it, and they do it over and over again without ever being made aware that they're making a mistake, or being forced to go back and redo it.

Earlier, we talked about the value of mistakes; that failure is a great teacher. But if you don't know that you're failing, you can't learn from it.

If you don't know that you're failing, you can't learn from it.

So I decided that I would give my students immediate feedback when they are in the learning phase.

This is the beauty of many of these online programs like KhanAcademy.org. They have you practice a skill, and then give you immediate feedback when you make an error. Not only does it tell you that you've made an error, but it shows you all the correct steps so that you can see where the mistake was made. Then you practice the skill over and over again until you get it right.

Which, again, is how you learn a skill.

When my students are working on learning a skill, they are given instant feedback on every question that they work on.

5 Teaching Norms that I abandoned

So there you go. Five more teaching norms that I decided to abandon, because I don't think they support growth and learning.

1. I give the students as long as they need on one skill before moving onto the next

2. I no longer penalize failure

3. I don't try to get through the entire curriculum with every student in one year

4. I celebrate success

5. I give instant feedback

In case you forgot, the first common practice that I gave up was whole group pacing – pushing all my students through the same skills at the same time. Instead, I focus on each student, where he needs work so that he can obtain growth.

Chapter 5 – Epiphany from Error

After realizing the numerous mistakes that I, as an educator, was making with my students (which I outlined in the previous chapter) I began to look for a new way of presenting material that allowed the following:

1. Differentiated instruction so no one is left behind

2. Give students as much time and practice as they need

3. Not penalize students for failure

4. Give Immediate Feedback

5. Celebrate success

As I contemplated how to implement my new philosophies, I was in the process of teaching long division to my 8th grade, Pre-Algebra students. I was very frustrated that they had not yet mastered this skill, and felt that, being an excellent teacher, I was the one to right this wrong.

After a few days of superb teaching with manipulatives, videos, and real-world examples, I assessed the students. Much to my dismay, there had been very few who had now mastered it. So I spent some more time on it, with similar results.

As I became more frustrated with them, for not knowing how to do this elementary task, several things occurred to me.

1. How often did I use long division in the real world? Honestly, I had worked in jobs outside of education, how often did I need to do long division? And when I did, how many times did I do it without busting out a calculator?

So I decided to stop taking everything so seriously.

2. These students were supposed to have learned long division years ago. So how many times had they been shown it before they were in my classroom? I'd bet that they had been shown hundreds, if not thousands of long division problems, yet they had not grasped it. Why did I consider

myself such a great teacher that I could do in weeks what others had not done in years?

So I realized that I'm not that special. And that the only way my students would ever learn long division was through a very long time of practice with instant feedback.

3. When did long division show up on the Pre-Algebra standardized test? The answer was almost never. There's some short division, like in two-step equations, but rarely do they have to do long division. So why was I spending so much time on this skill when both the students and I, the teacher, would not be evaluated on their comprehension of it on the end of year assessment?

So I decided to focus on the skills that they would be tested on.

4. Finally, and perhaps most revolutionary to me at the time, was the realization that they were not all struggling on "long division." Most of them were struggling on one of the steps in the process of long division.

For example, some didn't know their times tables, so they couldn't complete the first step. Some couldn't subtract with two or three digit numbers. Others had trouble tracking and weren't bringing the numbers down in the correct order or location. Not to mention what happened when we introduced decimals.

I realized that many math skills involved a series of steps performed in the correct order. If a student had not mastered all of the steps, they could not complete the final task.

In other words, some students needed to learn their multiplication tables, and some needed to learn how to subtract large numbers, and some needed to learn how to do short division, and others were ready to move on.

To truly reach all of them, and get growth, I needed to reach each one where they were.

I began to ponder this and realized that I could break the standard down into mini skills that needed to be mastered.

Like rungs on a ladder, each step needed to be completed so that the student could ascend to the top (completing the task at hand).

Math Problems are like LADDERS
if you *miss a step* it's hard to get to the top

HELP YOUR STUDENTS WITH
Learning Stations

RethinkMathTeacher.com

Chapter 6 – Plugging the Holes

Students often enter your classroom with holes in their repertoire of math skills. These holes often prevent them from being able to do the grade level work that you are assigning to them.

For example, students cannot do long division if they still don't know their times tables. Nor can they add fractions if they can't find the common denominator. Students can't graph a linear equation if they can't calculate the slope. Nor can they calculate the solution to the distance formula if they cannot add and subtract integers.

To help each student plug his/her hole, different students would be working on different tasks.

Consider all the skills involved in adding fractions:

The Problem	Step 1	Step 2	Step 3	Step 4	Step 5
$6\frac{1}{2} + 2\frac{1}{6} =$	$\frac{13}{2} + \frac{13}{6} =$	$\frac{39}{6} + \frac{13}{6} =$	$\frac{52}{6} =$	$8\frac{4}{6} =$	$8\frac{2}{3}$
SKILL:	Convert to Improper Fraction	Convert to Common Denominator	Add Fractions	Convert to Mixed Number	Simplify Fractions

Yes, there are different ways to solve this question. The point is that there are lots of skills needed to complete this one problem. And if the student has not mastered each skill, they will not get the correct answer.

So I decided to create a learning station for each skill and progress the students through the stations, one skill at a time, until they had mastered every skill on the list, and thus could complete the grade level work!

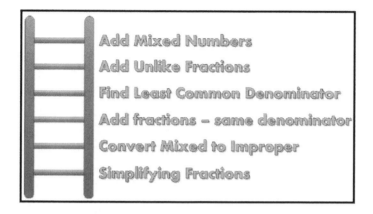

Students who didn't need work on one skill wouldn't be forced to do the work in that station but were free to progress to more advanced skills. Students who needed additional time or practice could be retained within that station for as long as they needed.

Since students would be working on different skills at the same time, the stations needed to all look the same for tracking purposes – and they needed to be able to be run independently.

In other words, the student should be able to do the work in that station without needing a teacher present to explain every step to him. This way I, the teacher, would be free to move around the classroom helping each student when they were truly stuck – yet the station would have the resources the student needed to relearn the skill and provide feedback without my presence.

The first thing I decided to do to help differentiate my instruction and reach each student where they were, was to break math skills down into prerequisite skills and then build a station for that individual skill. Then, I would progress the students through the stations until they mastered every skill and could thus do the grade level work.

For example: if my students were working on two step equations, I would build the following stations:

1. Adding Integers

2. Subtracting Integers

3. Multiplying and Dividing Integers

4. One Step Equations

5. Two Step Equations

If we were working on solving systems of equations by graphing, the stations would be:

1. Identifying and plotting points on the coordinate plane

2. Calculating slope

3. Graphing a linear equation

4. Solving a system of equations by graphing

Obviously, this is not the definitive list on these stations, and you can add, subtract, merge, or unmerge skills as you like. But my goal is to show you what some of the stations in my classroom look like, and how I list the prerequisite skills to help the students master the main skill.

Build Your Station: Homework #1

Look at the next (or current) topic that you are going to be teaching with your students. Solve a couple practice problems to get your mind thinking about the different steps involved in completing this task. Now list out all the prerequisite skills needed to complete the skill that your students will be working on. This chapter has a few examples that can illustrate this for you.

Each of the prerequisite skills you have listed out will become one learning station. You should also consider the sequencing of these stations – which one is first, second, etc.

For additional help with this homework assignment go to www.rethinkmathteacher.com/remediation-that-works. At the bottom of the page is a free worksheet to do this assignment and a video that demonstrates how to use the worksheet.

Section 2 – Building the Stations

Chapter 7 – An Overview

Before we dive into the nitty-gritty of the stations, how to create them, and how to best utilize them; and before we talk about implementation strategies and best practices; let's take a bird's eye view of what the learning stations are, how they function, and what the class looks like so that you can have a better idea of what we're building to impact all your students, helping each one grow.

The Purpose of the Station

We are going to build a station that the student can go into, independently or with a small group, that will reteach them the skill as well as give them a sufficient amount of practice with immediate feedback to truly master it.

The Prerequisite Stations

As we have discussed, many math concepts have prerequisite skills that you must be able to complete before you can perform the work. We've gone over several examples but think back to chapter two, where I shared how my Geometry students couldn't solve questions with the midpoint formula because they couldn't add integers.

In that example, adding integers would be the first station in a series of stations that culminates with the student being able to complete questions with the midpoint formula. Another prerequisite skill would be labeling a point on the coordinate plane since this too is needed to complete the midpoint formula.

So, for the skill of 'finding the midpoint,' I would have three learning stations. The first would be 'adding integers,' the second would be 'plotting and identifying points on the coordinate plane,' and the third would be 'finding the midpoint.' Obviously, the first and second can be in reverse order, and you might think there should be another station in there, but let's just use these three in this order for our example.

1. Adding Integers

2. Plotting and Identifying Points on the Coordinate Plane

3. Finding the Midpoint

No Prerequisite Skills

Some skills that you teach, don't really have prerequisite skills that are necessary to do the work. Like adding integers, or plotting points on a coordinate plane. In this case, you would just be building that one station. But it would still serve the purpose of remediation for students who were struggling on that standard.

Many Stations at the Same Time

So during class time, I could potentially have students working on all three stations at the same time, or more if my stronger students have mastered all three and have moved on to more advanced work.

Remember that the stations are designed to give the students several things:

1. As much time as possible

2. Lots of practice with immediate feedback

3. Confidence to do more advanced work – in part by not penalizing failure, in part by celebrating success

How do you Learn a New Skill?

Have you ever tried to learn something new? Whether it's playing a musical instrument, the proper technique in a sport, or something academic, there are several things that must happen for you to be able to learn the new skill and retain that information for an extended period of time.

When learning something new, the first thing that must happen is that you must have someone teach it to you. Whether that is an actual teacher, reading a book, or watching an instructional video, whenever you have tried to learn something new the first thing that has happened is that you have sought out instruction.

After being taught the new skill, you must practice it. However, it is not enough to merely practice it, you must also receive feedback to know whether or not you are completing the process correctly. It's also not enough to practice it a few times. To master a new concept, and have that knowledge convert to your long-term memory, you must practice it a sufficient amount of times. But not all people learn all skills with the same amount of practice.

Some of us are quick learners and can master the new skill with few repetitions. While others take more practice to master the concept. Too often in our educational system, we are not giving our weaker students sufficient practice, and that is why they are struggling to learn the concept. Many of our weakest students could become successful if they were just given the opportunity to have more practice, and to have that practice with feedback.

We will discuss these concepts more in Chapter 8. For now, we need our stations to do three things:

1. Give a Tutorial

2. Give Lots of Practice

3. Provide Immediate Feedback

Station Necessities

As we build these stations, we want them all to operate the same way, so that it is easy for you, the teacher, to track the students' progress.

Each station must also be able to be completed independently by the student. Many teachers make one of their stations a 'teacher led tutorial.' This will not work in the scenario we are discussing since your students will be working on different skills. Yet, all the students need a tutorial, considering they will all be working on a skill that they have not yet mastered.

The stations must not only have a tutorial section that is independent of the teacher, but it must also have lots of practice with instant feedback that is also not dependent upon the teacher. In other words, students must have a way of knowing whether or not they have answered each question correctly or not.

The student must also be able to work on that skill – stay in that station – for as long as she needs, and until she masters it. Furthermore, the station must have an accurate method for measuring student mastery.

Finally, the station must give LOTS of practice. As previously discussed, we learn through repetition. And it must be meaningful repetitions on the skill that we are developing, with instant feedback.

Three-Day Stations

We are going to build three-day stations that have a tutorial and lots of practice with instant feedback. At the end of the three days, the students will take a quiz on their station to determine whether or not they have mastered the skill. If they have not mastered it, they will repeat the station with different assignments (but on the same skill). If they have mastered it, they will move on to the next skill.

AN IMPORTANT NOTE

The stations do not replace quality instruction. The teacher is still necessary to do many things, including teaching. However, the stations are for differentiation, remediation, and acceleration.

Learning stations are for differentiation,
remediation, and acceleration.

Thus, the stations do NOT last the entire class period. They will last around twenty minutes each day (give or take a little depending on how the class is doing, and of course things always take longer when you are just starting them). We will discuss how to weave the station work into your class period in Chapter 14.

Station Appearance

The stations will all look the same because each day the students will be doing the same type of work. However they will all be doing the same work on a different skill.

The three-day station will consist of six tasks:

Task 1: A Tutorial

Task 2: Note Taking with the Tutorial

Task 3: Independent Practice with Immediate Feedback

Task 4: Independent Practice with Immediate Feedback (worksheet)

Task 5: Extension Activity

Task 6: An Assessment

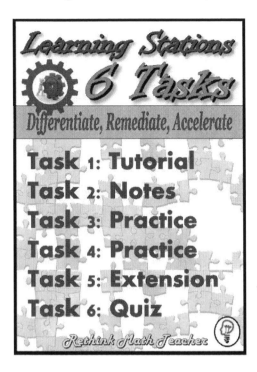

On Day 1 all students will complete their tutorial activity and take notes. The tutorial activity is where students are taught (or re-taught) how to do the work of the station. They must take notes during it so that they can reference it in the following days when they are working independently.

Day 2 and 3 are both independent practice with immediate feedback, which we will discuss in Chapter 8 in greater detail. The goal is for the student to get enough meaningful repetitions of work on the skill that they truly master it.

The extension activity is done after the students finish their independent work – so it can be done on Day 2 or Day 3. If it is not finished in class, it becomes homework. The extension activity is there, not only for extra practice, but also for your students who work at a faster pace than the majority of the class. It's also there to give at home practice and help prepare the student for the quiz.

At the end of the three-day station, there is a quiz to determine whether or not the student has mastered the skill. If the student has mastered that skill, they are promoted to the next station. If they have not mastered the skill, they are retained for another three-day rotation of the same station.

The quiz is done on the day after the three-day rotation. So it is technically the sixth task on Day 4. Besides giving the quiz on this day, you will also collect the student work from the three-day station and celebrate student success. Don't worry about collecting three days' worth of work from all your students, the grading process is very easy and you will be given several strategies in the chapters to come to help ease this burden.

Now let's take a closer look at each of these tasks.

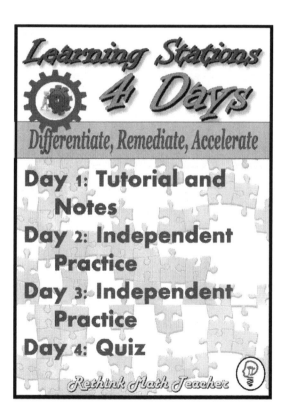

Chapter 8 – The 6 Tasks

Recently my daughters discovered the bracelet making loom. Have you seen these things? They're basically boards with pegs sticking up for you to wrap colored rubber bands around in different patterns. You then use a hooked instrument (or your fingers if you're really good) to pull the colored rubber bands around, or through, each other to create beautiful looking bracelets, necklaces, and other items.

Of course, my daughters had to have them and coaxed their grandmother into the purchase. Which meant that I now had to learn how to use this dreadful device.

My seven-year-old niece gave me my first lesson on how to create a bracelet using the loom. Though she was a great tutor, I couldn't remember all the steps once I tried to create one without her guidance. I was soon stuck trying to figure out what to do. Do I pull the orange one over the blue one? Or under it? ...Or through it?

What did I do when I could not figure out what to do? If I was at my niece's house, I would have asked her. But since I was now at home, just me and the loom, I pulled out the step-by-step directions and followed them. At several points during the construction, I would get stuck, or something wasn't working properly, and I would go back to the directions and re-read, trying to discover my error and how to fix it.

Eventually, I was successful and learned the skill.

My daughters then wanted to try some other bracelet designs that their cousins had shown them but for which we had no step-by-step instructions. So we went to YouTube and found a video of someone modeling it. We watched the video, pausing at important points, replaying other parts that were difficult, until we had mastered this as well.

You probably have similar stories to mine; where you tried to learn something new, but got stuck and needed a reteach. This is why we include a reteach in our stations.

Task 1 – The Tutorial

A Tutorial

The Learning Stations we have discussed are for students to maser one skill. It might be a new skill for them, or it might be a skill that they've already been exposed to but have not yet mastered. Either way, a tutorial is required.

There are multiple ways to teach – or reteach – a skill, as illustrated in the bracelet loom story.

Many teachers create a station where they sit with some of the students and give direct instruction as the tutorial. However, since we are using stations for differentiation, you are going to have students working on several different skills at the same time. So having the teacher give the instruction for all the stations is not practical. I recommend having the reteach activity of your learning station be something that the students can do independently, or in a small group, without needing the teacher's presence to guide them through the tutorial.

Remember that there are many different stations all being completed by different students at the same time. But, everyone is doing Task 1, regardless of what stations he or she is in. And Task 1 in every station is a tutorial.

Technology in the Classroom

If you have technology in the classroom, the reteach portion should be a tutorial video. You can find good, short teaching videos at VirtaulNerd.com, MathAntics.com, LearnZillion.com, and KhanAcademy.org.

If none of the above sites have what you're looking for you can always do a quick search online or even create your own and post it onto YouTube for free.

When I had a class set of laptops (one for every student) I purchased a class set of headphones so that each student could watch their tutorial video on their laptop and we didn't all have to listen to each other's devise. Of course, the students were welcome to bring their own headphones, but a class set of was fairly inexpensive and made life easy on me by having them in the room.

> Teacher Tip:
>
> The students will never all remember to bring in their headphones, just like they never all remember to do their homework. So purchasing a class set makes good sense. That way, if they forget them, they can always use yours.
>
> I purchased old school headphones that covered your ears – because sticking earbuds in your ears that have been in other people's ears, whom you don't even know, is just gross!
>
> The students still thought that these headphones were gross and would put them on over their jacket hood, or rip squares of paper to put between the headphones and their ears.

When I had less than a class set of laptops, I had to get creative. Normally, I could lump students together who were working on the same skill, and they could watch the video together. However, if grouping the students like this did not work, we would rotate the laptops during the period or on different days. Another option is to have some students work on the laptops this week while the rest of the class does the non-technology reteach, and then next week we switch – so everyone is using a laptop every other station rotation.

For the video tutorial, I would try to select one or two videos that totaled between 5 and 10 minutes in length.

I recommend putting these links into an online platform that's easy to navigate. Some schools have programs that can do this. However, if you are not so fortunate, you can use Google Classroom or Edmodo for free. If you don't like either of these, you can create a free webpage for your class at Wordpress or Wiz.

Regardless of what platform you choose to put your video links on, you want it to be very easy to navigate. So be sure to label sections and don't use a lot of words on the page. Just the name of the station, and then "Video 1," "Video 2," etc. is sufficient. Make sure to hyperlink all the video titles so that the students can easily get to the video that you want them to see.

Finally, make sure that you have students take notes while they watch the video. More on this in Task 2.

Edmodo

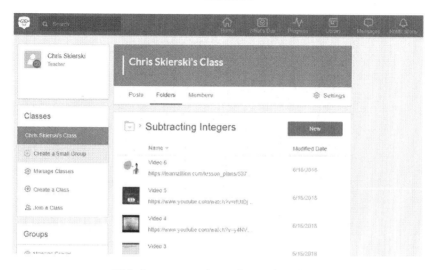

This is a screenshot of an Edmodo class.

After creating the class and having students enroll in it, Edmodo works like a social media platform. It allows you to send posts to your students, and you can also create folders like the ones above. This folder has many videos uploaded for tutorials on Subtracting Integers. I can also upload links to websites, documents, my own videos, images, and more. Edmodo also allows me to send reminders to students about what's due, as well as several other features that are helpful for a teacher.

Google Classroom

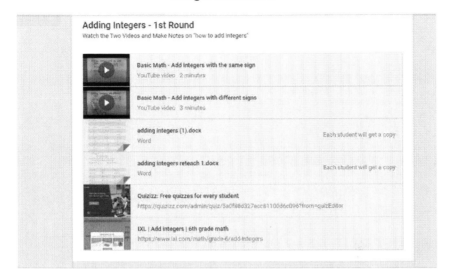

This is a screenshot of Google Classroom Folder

Notice that I have named the folder "adding integers – 1ˢᵗ round" – it is for students the first time they go through the adding integers station. If they don't pass, they will repeat the station, and find the folder labeled "adding integers – 2ⁿᵈ round."

I have two videos, which are the first two links. Below that are the worksheets which are actually in Google Docs, so the students can do them online if they like (or download them at home if they lost it or are absent). There are also links below those worksheets to the online assignments. You see that I have a Quizzizz (which is actually the extension) and an assignment in IXL.com. This information is also on the student's tracking paper which we will discuss in Chapter 10

Website

How to Add Integers

Video 1) (Same sign)

- https://www.youtube.com/watch?v=I2hcj8gg618

Video 2 (different signs)

- https://www.youtube.com/watch?v=Tre3Q5TuJdI

Video 4: VirtualNerd.com (adding same sign and opposite sign using number line)

- http://virtualnerd.com/middle-math/integers-coordinate-plane/add-integers/add-integers-number-line-example

Video 5 (adding integers, both, Flocabulary)

- https://www.flocabulary.com/unit/adding-integers/

Video 6: Math Anitcs, both

- https://www.youtube.com/watch?v=_BgbIvF90UE

Video 7 & 8: Learn Zillion

- https://learnzillion.com/lesson_plans/5250/lesson
- https://learnzillion.com/lesson_plans/5608-add-integers-using-chips

Video 9 & 10 Khan Academy

This is a screenshot of a website where I have linked the 10 tutorial videos for adding integers.

Notice that they are clearly titled with the video number, and the links are below, to try and help it be as easy as possible for the students to navigate.

No Technology in the Classroom

Of course, not all of us are fortunate enough to have technology in the classroom.

When I was in this situation, I would either use worksheets or the textbook for the tutorial task of the station work.

If the textbook had a good teaching section, I would use it for the tutorial section of their learning station. If the textbook tutorial was not so good, I would print (or create) a reteach worksheet, and print it for the students to read.

Again, no matter what method you use, the students must take notes during the tutorial section.

Task 1: Tutorial
Option 1: One laptop per student   - Watch one or two videos online, each student wears headphones
Option 2: Less than one laptop per student   - Group students together to watch videos on one laptop

Option 3: Less than one laptop per student
    - ½ class uses laptops and the other ½ uses textbook or worksheet
    - Next time we do task one, the two groups flip

Option 4: No laptops   - Everyone uses a worksheet or textbook for the tutorial

Build Your Station: Homework #2

Find the tutorials that you're going to be using for the stations that you outlined in Homework 1 (Chapter 6).

Either find the tutorial section in the notebook, print out a guided reteach from online, or find teaching videos that you can link to on the internet.

Record this information on a word document (either the pages in the textbook or copy and paste the links). Later we will put this all in one place for your students.

I have included a list of websites with good teaching videos or tutorials that you can print out for your stations. Get that resource www.rethinkmathteacher.com/reach-them-all-downloads.

Task 2 – Note Taking

The process of taking notes is a valuable skill. It helps with comprehension and retention. Students who take notes during class generally remember more, remember it longer, and understand it more completely.

Beyond that, notes are a valuable tool when a student is stuck on a problem. If they have taken good notes, they should be able to figure out how to complete the question that they are working on.

So make 'note taking' valuable.

The second task in each learning station is the completion of notes as they complete Task 1, the tutorial. Whether the student watches a video, completes a worksheet, or reads the examples in the textbook, they must take good notes.

I'm sure that you are aware that it is not always easy for a student to take good notes; especially in primary and middle grades. So spend some time teaching your students how to take good notes, and show them examples of what good notes look like.

I expect my students to accurately record the steps of the practice problems and explain the work in their notes. Sometimes, definitions are appropriate, as is labeling certain parts of a formula, equation, or another type of math problem.

But before I release my students to the task of note-taking, we practice it several times.

Before I release my students to the task of note taking, we practice it several times.

Rethink Math Teacher

Task 2 – Note Taking

The students should take notes as they read or watch the Task 1 tutorial. The students keep their notes for the entire three day period that they are working on that station, and then turn them in at the end of the station, on Day 4.

The reason that the students must keep their notes for the entire three-day cycle is so that they may reference them when they are completing the independent practice.

If a student raises their hand and asks me for help on his independent work, I review his notes with him and help him find how to do the work from his notes.

At this time, I will also write comments on his notes paper to help me with the grading at the end of the cycle. If he did not accurately record how to do one of the steps in his notes, I will write that information on the notes page and instruct him to go back to the tutorial and complete his notes. This way, when I am grading the notes, I can simply check the comments that I made on the paper and see if he completed it correctly.

If, when I am reviewing the student's notes with him, I recognize that he has done an excellent job with his notes, I put an A+ on the paper. This encourages him and makes grading a lot easier when I collect everyone's notes on Day 4.

If the student has 'misplaced' his notes, or never did them, I make him stop what he is working on, and return to task 1 and 2 – the tutorial and the note-taking – and redo them. I do this, in part, to make sure that the message is clearly understood that notes are valuable.

I don't have a worksheet that I give the students for their notes. I have them use a blank sheet of paper and expect them to take notes that are legible, helpful, and that explain the steps in a way that is easy to follow. I have seen some teachers make different templates for this, but it seems like extra work on the teacher, and I think it takes away from the student's ability to create notes on their own – which is a skill that I want them to become proficient at.

Day 1 – Two Tasks

The first day of the station is Task 1 and 2 – a tutorial and note-taking portion. This should take around 15-25 minutes. More on the timing of stations and the class structure in Chapter 14.

I do allow students to go on to the next task, which is the independent work if they finish Task 1 and 2 before time is done. This is because I want them to practice what they have just learned. However, the goal is to give enough time on Day 1 for everyone to complete Task 1 and Task 2, and it's okay if they don't get into Task 3.

| Day 1 | Task 1 – Tutorial |
| | Task 2 – Note-Taking |

Task 3 – Independent Practice with Immediate Feedback

I remember learning how to play the guitar. First, I was shown the correct finger position for a chord. Then I would press my fingers down in the same position as I had just been shown. I would check to see if I had done it correctly by strumming the guitar pick across the strings. Of course, the first time I tried to play a G, it sounded terrible. One finger was out of position, while another wasn't pushing hard enough down on the strings. So I had to reposition, push hard, and strum again. Eventually, after several attempts, the G chord was finally played correctly from the guitar that I was holding.

Then I would let go of the guitar strings and again attempt to grab the guitar the correct way to make the same sound again. After many attempts, eventually the G chord was learned, as were others, and from there more advanced skills were mastered.

When learning a musical instrument, you often instantly know if you have done it correctly because the correct sound has been made. Sometimes, it's not so easy to make the same determinations in math (and in other academic subjects). Which is why I recommend instant feedback when students do independent practice so that they know that they are doing the work correctly; or so that they can learn from their mistakes.

Task 3 and 4 – Independent Practice with Instant Feedback

To learn a new skill you must practice it repeatedly, and correctly.

Math teachers are really good at assigning independent practice, but often we are not so great about giving instant feedback. This is often because we are pacing the whole class together, and though everyone is working at different paces, the teacher is still trying to give feedback to everyone at the same time.

Practice loses its impact if it's done incorrectly. Imagine if I had continued playing the guitar the same way I had done the first time I tried to play it? What if I thought that was correct and had repeated it hundreds, or even thousands, of times. When I played the guitar it would sound terrible – but I would not know it.

Math is not always as easy to realize that you've made a mistake, and if it's not corrected, the learner will continue making that mistake over and over again, until it's engraved in their mind that this is the proper way to do the problem – thus reinforcing a bad habit.

This is why feedback is so vital. When the student makes a mistake and immediately recognizes it, he is forced to go back and reevaluate the work, search for the cause of the error, and correct it.

Immediate feedback is vital to correctly learning a skill

Task 3

If you have technology in the classroom, immediate feedback is easy. You are able to assign work to your students on online platforms like Khan Academy, IXL, AAAmath, MathIsFun, and other websites where the students are immediately made aware that they have made a mistake.

So for Task 3, if I have technology in the classroom, I assign work on an online platform like the ones mentioned above. If none of those are available to me, I will make a Google quiz that gives instant feedback. The advantage of these is that students are first given the problem and then they immediately are told whether they got it right or not. And most of these websites offer explanations so that the student can learn from their mistake.

Teacher Tip

IXL is a paid service, but you can try it for free for 30 days, which I do recommend. All you need is an email address. Once signed up, you create your student accounts (I just add their first name and last initial) and give them a password. To make the password process easier, I give all my students the same password. IXL creates a standard username so it becomes very easy for everyone to remember how to login. IXL has a teacher page that will show you your students' results, so the students don't need to show you how many points they earned.

If you do not utilize this option, it is very easy for the students to hit a couple buttons on the keyboard, especially in Google Chrome, and change the score on their screen. So they will show you that they earned 100 points, when in fact they haven't done any of the work. But no fear, simply logging into your teacher page will mitigate this cheating temptation.

Khan Academy's teacher page is a little more involved when trying to setup your student accounts. However, it's free. It too shows you your student results on your teacher page. So if you have set it up correctly, with everyone having their own login, checking student work becomes easy.

At the time of this writing, AAAmath and Math is Fun do not offer logins and usernames. Thus, when the student completes the work, they must show it to you. There are many other websites out there that can do the same, however, they typically have a fee associated with them.

No Technology in the Room

If you do not have technology in the classroom, you can use worksheets or textbook work as the independent practice and provide or create your own answer sheets so that the student can check their work when they have completed each problem.

I have done several things to help with this endeavor. The first is that I have put both the worksheet and the answer sheet in a folder, and the folder is labeled with the station that the students are working on. I then put all those folders on a shelf in one section of the classroom, so finding the worksheets and answer sheets are easy to do.

Another trick I have done, but this one does take a bit more time, is that I have one problem and the work for it, with the answer, on an index card. That card is then put in an envelope and labeled with the question number. This way, students can check each problem after they have completed it and aren't tempted to cheat by looking at the answers to other problems on the worksheet before they have done the work for them.

The trick is to try to emphasize to the students that the answers are provided, so there's no need to cheat. It is in their best interest to do the work and then check the answers so that they are truly comprehending the material – otherwise, they are skipping the learning process.

Yes, invariably, you will have students who still try to take shortcuts and cheat on the work since the answers are provided. But the beauty of doing learning stations the way we have outlined in this book is that at the end of the three-day station there is an assessment. If students haven't truly grasped the material, they will not pass the assessment, and they will have to do the station work again. So, in the end, cheaters don't win and you as the teacher must stress this to the students.

I would not let the possibility of cheating deter you from providing instant feedback, which is so important to the learning process.

Conclusion

Task 3 is independent practice with immediate feedback. Ideally, this is done online. However, it can still be accomplished using worksheets or even the textbook. Make sure that you simplify the process of finding work for the student as much as possible. You can put links to the online assignments under the video links on your online platform. Or, if you are using worksheets, you can put them in a folder in an obvious place in the classroom.

Day 1	Task 1 – Tutorial
	Task 2 – Note-Taking
Day 2	Task 3 – Independent Practice *(preferably online)*

Build Your Station: Homework #3

Find independent practice for Task 3 of your learning station(s). If you are going to do it online, which is recommended, decide which website you are going to use. I do recommend IXL or Khan Academy as first choices. If you are using one of those, also set up your teacher page and student accounts.

If you are not doing online work, select the textbook section or worksheet for the independent practice, and generate answer sheets or cards. Put them in a folder that is labeled with the name of the station.

Task 4 - Independent Practice with Immediate Feedback

On the third day of the Learning Station, students complete Task 4, which is just like Task 3 – independent practice with immediate feedback. However, for logistical purposes, I do not offer a technology option for Task 4 – it's either in the textbook or it's a worksheet.

Remember that the key to mastering a new concept is good teaching and meaningful repetitions. These repetitions help the learner retain the new knowledge longer, and master it more completely. This is the reason that Task 3 and 4 are both independent practice – so the students get lots of quality attempts.

Thus Task 4 is another independent practice with instant feedback.

I prefer not to do this one online. There are a few reasons why I use a textbook or a worksheet instead of another online practice activity.

First, if I don't have enough technology devices in the classroom, having Task 3 online and Task 4 offline allows me to split the class in half. Then the lack of devices in not an issue. So, on Day 2 half of the class has laptops and is doing Task 3, the online practice, while the other half does Task 4 – a textbook assignment or worksheet. Then, on Day 3, we flip. So everyone is online one day and not online the other day.

Limited Technology		
Independent Practice		
	½ of Class	½ of Class
Day 2	Task 3 Online	Task 4 Textbook or Worksheet
Day 3	Task 4 Textbook or Worksheet	Task 3 Online

The next reason I like using paper and pencil for Task 4 is that it allows me to see the students' work. As you math teachers well know, there is great value in seeing a student's work when they are struggling with a concept. Often, reviewing their work reveals their thought processes and misconceptions.

When a student has answered a question incorrectly and I, as the teacher, come to help them, often I can evaluate their work and discover the error that they're making.

The third reason I like a non-technology driven activity for Task 4 is that I believe that there is value in writing and working on paper. The process of interpreting symbols as words and numbers and then analyzing them, and reinterpreting them into new symbols is a healthy activity for the brain, and I want to foster this with my students.

Finally, if a student is absent on one of the days of the station work, and I'm trying to get them caught up, taking home a worksheet or some problems out of the textbook is an easy task. Not all of my students have internet or a computer and are thus unable to do the makeup work at home to catch up with the missing work.

Teacher Tip

4 Reasons Task 4 is not Online

1) It helps when technology is limited in the classroom

2) The teacher can review students' work

3) The writing process has value

4) Makeup work is easier

Task 4 is on Day 3, which is the last day of the station. On Day 4 the students will take a quiz to determine whether or not they have mastered the skill of the learning station that they are working on. But there's still one more task…

Day 1	**Task 1 – Tutorial**
	Task 2 – Note-Taking
Day 2	**Task 3 – Independent Practice** *(preferably online)*
Day 3	**Task 4 - Independent Practice** *(preferably offline)*

Build Your Station: Homework #4

For each learning station that you are creating, select your Task 4, independent practice assignment. Use the section of the textbook or a worksheet.

Print the worksheet and the answer key and put them both in the folder with the station name on it. If you are using the textbook practice, you may not need to print an answer key if the answers are in the back of the book. However, if they are not, or you would like to show the work with the problems, you should create that worksheet and put it in the station folder.

Task 5 – The Extension

Just to recap, the stations last three days. The first day is Task 1 and 2 – a tutorial and note taking. Day 2 is Task 3 – independent work, preferably online. Day 3 is also independent work, but I prefer it to be a physical product like a worksheet or work from the textbook. Task 5 is an extension activity, but it is not done on Day 4 – because the station is only three days long.

Task 5 is an extension activity serves two purposes. First, in case the student finishes the work of the station quickly and has nothing to do with the remaining time, they may work on the extension activity. Second, it is also supposed to function as a preparation for the quiz that they will take on Day 4.

For the extension activity, I normally give a worksheet. Originally, it was just a regular worksheet with lots of practice problems. But recently, I have started using worksheets that have an activity embedded into them – like a color by numbers or a maze – so that each step in the completion of the activity involves correctly answering the math question, and the student will know that she is doing it correctly because when she colors everything properly, a picture appears; or because she got to the end of the maze.

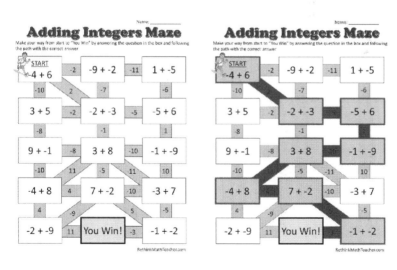

The extension activity is due on Day 4, so for most of my students, it's homework. Now, I do not give a lot of homework, nor am I a big fan of an abundance of homework. But I rationalize it by telling myself that in the three days of station work they only have one worksheet that is homework, and that's only if they don't finish it in class.

Also, for the extension activity, I don't feel compelled to give instant feedback. Part of the reason is that after three days of work, they should have mastered the skill, and on the next day they are going to be assessed so they should be able to do the work by now. Furthermore, if some of my students are not completing it in the class, they will not have the advantage of the instant feedback since they will be doing the work at home. So I'm not going to further incentivize them to race through their station work just so they can do the extension in class, and have the benefit of the answer sheets.

Day 1	Task 1 – Tutorial	Task 5 – Extension Activity
	Task 2 – Note-Taking	
Day 2	Task 3 – Independent Practice *(preferably online)*	
Day 3	Task 4 - Independent Practice *(preferably offline)*	

Build Your Station: Homework #5

Find an extension activity for your station that the student can do independently, and can complete at home. I usually select a creative worksheet.

Task 6 – The Quiz

Throughout this book, I have given several examples of learning a skill: shooting a basketball, playing the guitar, riding a bicycle, and snowboarding. All of these types of skills have some type of assessment built into them so that the student knows that she is performing them correctly.

Strum a guitar while pressing on the right strings in the right position – get a musical note!

Shoot the ball with the right aim and distance – it goes in the hoop!

Balance correctly while pedaling on a bicycle – you don't fall down!

Turn a snowboard perpendicular to the slope and lean back – you stop!

I realize that these are all limited examples, but the point remains that you can assess your mastery. Mathematics isn't always as obvious to the learner. Which is why an assessment is necessary to determine mastery.

In Chapter 4 we discussed that we must expect mastery. Too often, in traditional education, students are promoted from one skill to the next without true mastery. One of the wonderful things about using learning stations the way that we have outlined in this book is that we can expect mastery without penalizing failure. If the student does not pass the assessment, they simply do another three-day rotation of that skill's station. And since the entire class is differentiated – with different students working on different skills all at the same time; when the student is retained on that standard, it is not detrimental to the progress of the other students in the class.

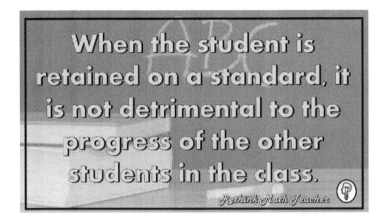

When the student is retained on a standard, it is not detrimental to the progress of the other students in the class.

Rethink Math Teacher

The Assessment

On the fourth day of the station, I administer an assessment to measure the student's comprehension of the skill that they've been working on. I recommend making the quiz simple and direct.

I typically give between 12 and 25 questions depending on how involved the skill is. So long division with decimals or two-step equations would have fewer questions because there are more steps involved in completing the work, and the students will take longer to finish. Conversely, adding integers or plotting points on a coordinate plane are much simpler tasks (in that there are not many steps involved), so they would have more problems on the quiz.

Also, I strongly recommend that the quiz is only on the skill that they've been working on, with no trick questions. So if the learning station is on simplifying fractions, the quiz should just have those type of questions. No curveballs, where the students first have to convert from a mixed number or set the problem up as a proportion. Make the assessment reflect the skill that they have been focusing on in the station.

---

*Make the assessment reflect the skill that they have
been focusing on in the learning station.*

I also don't give word problems on the assessment, unless that was the
skill that they were working on in the station. If the skill was on one step
equations, the quiz will have 16 to 20 questions that all look like:

1) x + 2 = -8   2) -20 = -4x   3) -2 – x = 9

If I want them to work on solving one step equations with word problems,
I will make that the station that they work on after they complete solving
one step equations, because they must be able to do the algebra before
they can complete the word problems.

Administration of the Assessment

On Day 4, all students take the assessment – regardless of the station that
they're working on – regardless of how many days they missed this week.
I give a set amount of time to complete the assessment, normally between
15 and 20 minutes. As the students complete the assessment, I collect it
from them. Since it is a short assessment, I can quickly grade it. My goal is
to grade all of them in class so that I can announce their results before the
end of the period.

Collecting Student Work – Closing the Station

After the student has turned in his quiz, his job is to get out his three or
four documents from this station which are also due. (In case you need a
quick recap, those documents are Task 2 – their notes, task 4 – the
independent practice, Task 5 - the extension, and possibly Task 3 –
independent work if it was not done online. All of these documents are
attached to the student tracking form, which we will discuss in chapter
ten.)

I have them do this after the quiz so that I have extra time in class to grade the quizzes, as I try to complete this before the end of the period (or day), so that we can do our promotions.

Day 1	Task 1 – Tutorial	Task 5 – Extension Activity
	Task 2 – Note-Taking	
Day 2	Task 3 – Independent Practice (preferably online)	
Day 3	Task 4 - Independent Practice (preferably offline)	
Day 4	Task 6 – Quiz and Promotions	

Here's an example of what my adding integers quiz looks like. I use boxes around the problems so that it's easy to find their answers. It's labeled "Quiz 1" because I make 3 similar quizzes for each station so that when the student repeats the station, he has a different quiz to do. Finally, notice that there are no word problems or trick questions. The station

Name: _____

Adding Integers Quiz 1

6 + (-8)	-9 + 5	14 + (-3)	-7 + 12
-3 + (-2)	-4 + (-4)	8 + (-8)	(-5) + (-12)
4 + 5	-7 + 1	13 + (-3)	-5 + 14
-2 + 2	8 + 13	(-4) + (-9)	-3 + 11
-19 + 11	-6 + (-3)	2 + (-17)	-11 + 9

was on adding integers and I am only assessing their ability to complete this task. Other skills, like determining which operation to use in a word problem or whether the number in the word problem is positive or negative are handled at a different time: either in a different station or during whole group time.

Build Your Station: Homework #6

Create a short quiz on the skill being done in your station(s).

Chapter 9 – Celebrate Good Times, C'mon!

On the fourth day of the learning station, the students take their quiz. But we do not call it "Quiz Day," we call it "Promotion Day," and it is their favorite day!

I try to grade the quizzes as they are turned in and with the remaining time in class. Because they're such short assessments, I usually can.

As previously discussed, mastery is expected. I set the bar for mastery at 80%.

If the student scores an 80% or better on the assessment, I consider that proficient, and she is *promoted* to the next station. If she does not score above an 80%, she is retained in the station for another rotation.

After a student finishes her quiz, she must turn it into me and then get her papers together from the three-day station to turn in. While students are doing that, I try to grade everyone's quiz.

Once I have graded all the quizzes, which is usually the same day as the quiz, we do the 'promotions.' If I don't finish grading that day, we do it the first thing on the next day.

Here's what I do to make it a "Promotion Day."

I play music. Normally it's the song, "We are the Champions" by Queen. The students are allowed to pick another song that they would prefer, it simply must be school appropriate. However, no one ever brings me an alternative song, and we always settle on Queen.

As we listen to this classic celebratory song, I read the names of the students who passed their quiz with an 80% or better. The entire class claps for that student, who then gets out of her seat and puts her name under a banner to commemorate her success. The banner has the name of the station that she just completed. She has already written her names on an index card, which is then placed under that banner, commemorating her success. More on the pennants in Chapter 10.

Monuments

Academic success should be a big deal. So celebrate your students' success.

The bigger a deal that you make it, the more pride your students will take in their accomplishments. So music, clapping, and name under a banner are all a great start. To go a step further, you could send a certificate home, so that their parents could also continue the celebration.

They'll think it's too cheesy

Yes, your students will tell you it's corny and a bit embarrassing. And for some, it might be. However, I was doing this at a Title 1 middle school, and they loved it... even if they pretended not to.

As I mentioned earlier, promotion day was their favorite. Every day, when they entered my class they would ask me, "is it promotion day?" Even though we had just had one the day before, and they knew it was a four-day rotation. They did this because they enjoyed being celebrated, and they enjoyed the feeling of being successful – which every student should have the chance to feel.

What if they don't pass?

Obviously, not all of your students will pass the station each time you do an assessment. Those who passed are recognized and then moved on to the next station – which I will explain a bit more in chapter ten and eleven. For those who don't pass, I don't call their names out or try to embarrass them in any way. I do return their quizzes to them so that they can see the mistakes they made and try to learn from them as well.

On the next day – the day *after* the quiz and promotion day – we begin Day 1 of the next three-day learning station. Those who passed the assessment are beginning a new station. Those who did not pass their quiz, are retained in the same station. In the next chapter, you will see a little better what that looks like.

Extra Support

Students who did not pass the station may need some extra support. So when a student repeats a station (especially if they repeat it more than once) I try to partner them with another student. This may be a student who speaks the same language if the student's first language isn't English, or it may be another student working on the same station so that they can work together. Sometimes, I even partner them with a student who is very far ahead so that the stronger student may help teach the struggling one.

Of course, I try to work more with these students as much as possible, but that it is not always feasible, so I utilize my students to help me with this matter.

Build Your Station: Homework #7

How will you celebrate your students' success? I do recommend banners on the wall for them to put their names under. But is there anything else you that you think would be fun and appropriate for your class?

Chapter 10 – The Pennants

As mentioned, I have pennants on the wall that label the stations in the order that they will be completed by the students. As the student masters a station, they put their name under the appropriate pennant.

This is part of the celebration, but it also helps me, the teacher, keep track of where all my students are. It also is appreciated by administrators who like data.

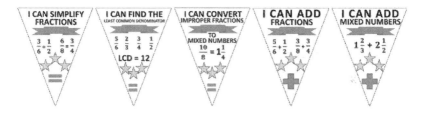

The image above is an example of what the pennants might look like, as well as the order that they would be placed in.

Teacher Tip

I have students make their name tags when they have finished a quiz and are sitting there with nothing to do. They're given an index card (or half an index card) and must write their name legibly. They may decorate it however they see fit.

If I am doing this with multiple classes, I will use different colored index cards (or just different colored paper cut into small squares) for each class. This is so that I can easily see who is in what station for each class.

Teacher Tip

I used to print colored pennants, like the ones above, because they looked nice. But then I started printing them in black and white and giving them to the students to color for extra credit. I often give several black and white pennants to different students in the class (of the same skill) and we vote on whose is the best.

They look so much nicer when the students color them in, and it's more fun. Plus it creates some student buy-in.

Build Your Station: Homework #8

Create your own pennants and decide where on your wall you will be hanging them.

I create these pennants in PowerPoint. It is a free download www.rethinkmathteacher.com/reach-them-all-downloads.

In it are several pennants already completed for you. You can also use it as a template to create your own.

Chapter 11 – Putting it all Together

Let's quickly recap what the three-day station looks like:

Day 1	Task 1 – Tutorial	Task 5 – Extension Activity
	Task 2 – Note-Taking	
Day 2	Task 3 – Independent Practice *(preferably online)*	
Day 3	Task 4 - Independent Practice *(preferably offline)*	
Day 4	Task 6 – Quiz and Promotions	

Now that you have a good handle on this, the trick is that you want your students to be able to navigate the learning station in a quick and easy manner. First, you don't want the students spending a lot of time trying to figure out what website to log in to, or which task they're supposed to be working on, because you want them spending as much time as possible practicing the math concept. Furthermore, since everyone's working on a different skill at the same time, you won't be able to assist each student with trying to figure out what task they're on and where it's located.

So the key is to compile all the work for that station in one place so that it is easy for the students to understand and follow. Also, if the students are doing work online, you want all that work in an easy-to-find location so that they can click on a link and immediately be taken to the video that you want them to watch or to the exercise you want them to complete.

The Station Tracker

To begin, I create a form that the students keep with them as long as they are working on that station. See below:

ADDING INTEGERS STATION				
Task	Title	Date	Notes	Initial
1	Watch Video 1 and 2			
2	Take Notes with Video			
3	IXL.com - N.2 Add Integers		70 pts	
4	Add Integers 1 - Worksheet			
5	Add Integers Reteach 1 - Worksheet			
QUIZ 1				

This is only the top portion of the worksheet, which we will now dissect.

You notice that the five tasks are listed out in order, and labeled accordingly (the sixth task is the quiz). There is also a column for the date that they completed it, a note section, and their initials. I have them write their score in the notes section – which should always be a 100% because answer sheets are provided. In the case of task 3, I only want the student to get 70 points on the IXL assignment, so I pre-fill that in for the student.

For the first task, it just reads 'watch video 1 and 2,' it doesn't list the video names or web addresses. This is because I put all the videos on an online platform. So the student merely needs to log into that platform, find the station that he's working on (in this case 'adding integers station') and click on video 1 and video 2. From that website, each video has a hyperlink which immediately take the student to the video.

One more note before moving on. Task 4 and 5 are worksheets. On the student tracker page, I list the title of the worksheet. I usually title them with a number, like "Adding Integers W.S. 1" (W.S. = worksheet).

In the classroom are folders, labeled with the different stations. When you open up that folder, the student will find the different resources that they need for their station, including the worksheets and the answer keys. Everything is labeled so that the student can easily find what they are looking for.

Teacher Tip

Remember that we spoke about where to host these videos at length in Chapter 8, Task 1. There I showed you screenshots of an Edmodo class, a Google Classroom Assignment, and a website that you could create for free at www.wordpress.com

Wherever you place your videos, you should also include hyperlinks to the online assignments so that you can just put the words "watch video 1" on the online platform, and the students can click the link. It can say the same on the student tracking form.

Round 2

As already mentioned, if the student does not demonstrate proficiency on the skill in that station – by passing the quiz on Day 4 – they are retained in that station for another three-day rotation. So I include this information on the Station Tracker.

Task	Title	Date	Notes	Initial
ADDING INTEGERS STATION				
1	Watch Video 1 and 2			
2	Take Notes with Video			
3	IXL.com - N.2 Add Integers		70 pts	
4	Add Integers 1 - Worksheet			
5	Add Integers Reteach 1 - Worksheet			
QUIZ 1				
Round 2				
1	Watch Video 4			
1	Take Notes with Video			
2	Khan Academy - Adding Integers			
3	Add Integers 2 - Worksheet			
4	Add Integers Reteach 2 - Worksheet			
QUIZ 2				
Round 3				
1	Watch Video 7-8			
2	Take Notes with Video			
3	www.MathGame.com: Adding Integers			
4	Add Integers 3 - Worksheet			
5	Add Integers Reteach 3 - Worksheet			
QUIZ 3				

The station tracking form should make it obvious where each round begins and ends. As you know, even though you make something very obvious to your students you will still have to train them to notice it.

Also, each 'Task 1' is a different video, each worksheet is different, each online practice is different, for the different rounds. As you know, students will often say "we already did this," when they are doing something again, even if they didn't grasp it the first time. But this is human nature, we're all the same way. So to help combat this, I spend a little extra time selecting different activities for each task.

I build this form in Microsoft Excel, but a free template is available at www.rethinkmathteacher.com/reach-them-all-downloads.

What if they don't master the skill after the third round?

There are some students who will not master the skill after three rounds of working on it, for whatever reason. When this happens, remember that we are focused on growth, and the goal is mastery. So we are not going to push them on to the next skill. Nor are we going to give up on them.

There are several options listed below for what you can do when you have a student who is struggling more than most on a station and just can't seem to master it.

Option 1 is to send the student back to the previous station. Since they already passed it once, they should be able to complete the task, and thus build up their confidence.

Option 2 is to spend some extra time evaluating their work to discover the error that they are making, and put them in a station that will help them work on that skill. For example, if the station is on adding mixed numbers, and you realize the student keeps messing up on converting his improper fraction back into a mixed number after he has done all that work, then you could put him in the appropriate station to help fix the mistake he keeps making.

Option 3 is to have a stronger student work with the struggling student so that the stronger student may help teach her the skill.

Teacher Tip

When I have done option three, and assigned a stronger student as a teacher to the weaker one, I offered the stronger student extra credit if they do such a good job teaching the weaker one that she passes the station. But this has often ended with the stronger student putting a lot of pressure on the weaker one, or even getting really mad at them when they did not pass it. So instead, I offered the stronger student extra credit or some other incentive merely for helping,

---

All three options listed above can and have worked. You should decide which is best based on your student, the standard, the class, and any other factors you feel are important.

Build Your Station: Homework #9

Download the student tracking form at the link below or create your own. Fill in the five tasks for your learning station.

http://www.rethinkmathteacher.com/reach-them-all-downloads/,

Then, put that information on an online platform (again, I recommend Google Classroom or Edmodo).

Finally, print out all the worksheets, answer sheets, and the student tracking form for your station. Put all of those in one folder. Print a label for that folder and put it in a designated section of your classroom.

Chapter 12 – Pre Test and Motivation

In Chapter 6 we looked at a skill that you're about to teach to your students. We also considered the various prerequisite skills that the student needed to be able to do to complete the grade level work – and it might have been no prerequisite skills.

This was also your homework assignment #1.

For example, if the skill is finding the area of composite figures. The students must be able to find the area of rectangles, find the area of triangles, and find the area of circles and semi-circles (assuming the composite figure can be made of those shapes).

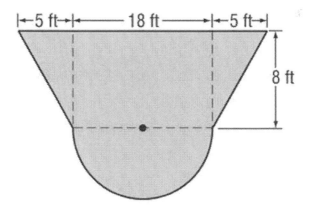

A composite figure is made up of different shapes

So maybe you make this the three stations for this skill:

1) Area of rectangles and triangles

2) Area of circles and semicircles

3) Area of composite figures

Teacher Tip:

One of the hardest parts of solving the area of composite figures, for students, is identifying the length of a side not given. That might be an excellent fourth station, or the act of identifying the missing side length could be an excellent whole group activity with guided practice and think-out-louds.

You have now taken one skill and broken it into three stations. Obviously, you probably have a different skill and have a different number of stations, but we'll continue using the example above to make the point.

You have selected five tasks for each station and made a quiz. You've also organized all of this information on a student tracking form. And you have placed all this information online (if you have technology in the classroom) and in folders.

Finally, you've created a pennant for each stations and hung them on the wall.

Before you are ready to begin implementing these wonderful stations in your class, you should create a Pre-Test so that you know which students should be in which station?

The Pre-Test should assess the student's ability to do each of the 3 tasks above. My pretest for the above three stations would look like this:

The pretest is longer than the quiz that the students will take at the end of the station, so I allow a longer period of time to finish, and I don't try to grade it in class before the end of the day.

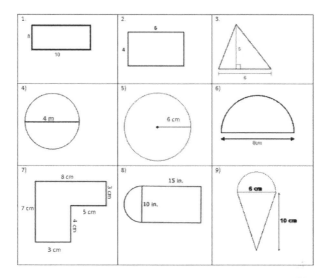

If you look at the quiz I exampled on the previous page, you will notice that it is divided into three sections. Questions 1-3 all are on the 'area of rectangles and triangles,' which we said would be my first station. Questions 4-6 are assessing 'circles and semi-circles,' which would be Station 2. And the last three questions are on the area of composite figures, which would be my third station.

> **Teacher Tip:**
>
> Make sure you are very familiar with your standards. You don't want to spend time on teaching composite figures with semi-circles or triangles if the standard tells you that the students will not be assessed for on composite figures with semi-circles. Only build stations on what the students are required to know based on the standards.

Incentivize

Before handing the quiz to the students, I let the students know that we're about to take a test. I explain to them that this test is actually three tests in one! I further explain that I will use the information from this test to place them into their learning stations that they will begin on the next school day.

To motivate them to do well, I give these two bonuses which the students really like.

First, I let them know that since the test is three tests in one, they will be receiving three test grades on this one assessment. So they could have three A's in the grade book by the end of the day.

Second, I explain to them that I will not enter any grade into the book that is lower than an 80%. So if they completely bomb the quiz and don't get any questions right, I will not put a grade in the book – so this test cannot hurt their grade in any way.

Both of these motivators are my attempt to get them to work their best on the assessment so that I can truly see where their needs are; and I tell them this up front.

I know that many schools are getting away from grades, so this may not apply to you. But for the many schools that still are, this is my recommendation.

If you are not using grades, the stations and their assessments are how you will measure student proficiency.

When the students have finished their assessment, I hand them three index cards and instruct them to write their name on each card and color it. They may write their name creatively, as long as it's legible, and they can do each card differently. These three cards are for them to put under the banners on the wall after they have mastered each of the three stations.

Scoring the Assessment

If the student misses any of questions 1-3, they are in the first station, and I put a mark on their paper that says the same.

If, however, they got all 1-3 correct, and they missed one or more of the questions in 4-6, I put a *100%* over questions 1-3 and let the student know that they are on the second station. I do the same for questions 7-9.

If the student got all 3 sections correct, I put *100%* on their paper three times.

The next school day, I hand the students their Student Tracker form for the station that they will be working on based on the results of their pre-test. I also have students put their name tags under each banner that they tested out of by getting a 100% on.

Example 1

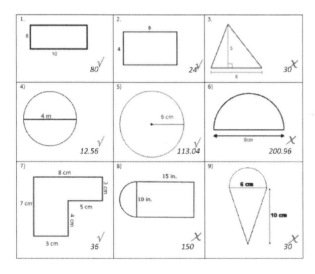

Example 2

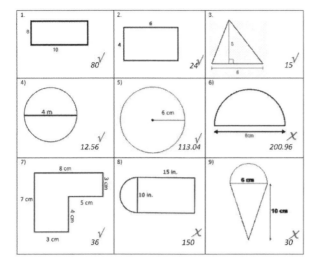

In Example 1, the student missed questions in all three sections, so she will be placed in the first learning station, area of rectangles and triangles. In Example 2, the student correctly answered every question in the first section. So she would get a 100% for area of rectangles and triangles, and would not need to do that learning station. She would also put her name under that banner. However, she missed one question on the second section, area of circles and semi circles. So she would be working on that station.

Build Your Station: Homework #10

You've already mapped out the prerequisite skills for the standard you are working on. So you know how many stations you will be implementing.

Create a pre-test, with a few questions for each station.

Chapter 13 — A Checklist

You are now ready to begin!

You have broken your standard down into prerequisite skills!

You've assigned five tasks and a quiz to each of those skills, which is its own assessment!

You created a pre-test to assess which students belong in which station!

And... you have beautiful pennants hanging on the wall to celebrate your students' success! Before you begin, let's just make sure you have everything setup that you need.

Make sure that you have the following for EACH station you created:

- ☐ A student tracking form
- ☐ A pennant on the wall to celebrate success
- ☐ Your videos online OR the tutorial worksheet printed
- ☐ Your Task 3 assignment - either online or a worksheet
- ☐ Your Task 4 worksheet
- ☐ Answer sheets for all your worksheets
- ☐ A Task 5 extension activity or worksheet
- ☐ All the worksheets and answer sheets in one folder in a designated area of the classroom
- ☐ A quiz
- ☐ A pre-test that will place the students in the stations
- ☐ Index cards for each student to write their name on
- ☐ Certificates to send home (optional)

One more note, make sure you print enough copies of everything to last you a while.

Chapter 14 – Implementation

After you have all of your stations set up; all the papers printed and in a folder, an online platform to store links to videos and online assignments, and pennants on the wall, you are now ready to have a successful learning station.

Here's how to implement.

Before Day 1 – Pre-Test

On the very first day, you have to explain to students what this is going to look like. So talk to them about the tasks, the breaking down of the standards, the different stations at the same time, and the philosophy that they are expected to master concepts – they will no longer be left behind.

You should also spend some time reviewing how to take notes. Show a video of a skill that everyone can work on, and have the students take notes on it. Guide them through the note-taking process, pointing out best practices and things to avoid.

Finally, on this very first day, the students must all take the pre-test that you made in Chapter 11. Remember to explain to the students that the pre-test counts as multiple test grades, but only if they do well on it. It will not count against them if they don't do well on it. It's also to determine what station they'll be in.

When students have finished their pre-test, have them create their name tags that will go on the wall underneath the banners when they master a skill. I like to use index cards, but they do take up a lot of room, so feel free to use smaller strips of paper or something else creative.

The First Day 1

After the pre-test day is complete, the next day is the first Day 1 of the learning stations.

Make sure to hand everyone their Station Tracker form for the station that they're working on. You should also have students put their names under the pennants of the stations that they tested out of. This way you can look at the wall and immediately know who is working on what station.

It's important on this day to walk students through the process of working through the station. So show them how to get onto the online platform to find the videos they're supposed to watch, remind them how to take notes and that they need to keep them for the entire three days. Also, show them where the folders are with the worksheets and answer sheets, and remind them how to use the answer sheet properly.

As a teacher, you know that the first few times you do something, you have to spend more time than normal establishing routines and reminding students where everything is and how everything is supposed to operate. But if you do this effectively, after the first few days, it will run very smoothly and effortlessly.

Remember that all students are doing a tutorial and taking notes on Day 1. So set this up as we have already discussed in Chapter 8, under Task 1. If you can get everyone on a laptop with headphones, great! If you have to partner up, do so. But if everyone's working out of the textbook or half the room is working out of the textbook and half are online, that's okay too.

If the student finishes Task 1 and 2 – the tutorial video and the notes – before station time is complete on Day 1, they may move on to Task 3, the independent practice.

At the end of the station time, after everyone has cleaned up and is back in his or her seat, you need to go over the student tracking form with them. Everyone should date and initial Task 1 and 2, showing that he or she completed that task on this day's date. If they began Task 3 but did not finish it, they shouldn't initial or date Task 3, because it's incomplete. Have them write a 100% for Task 1, the tutorial. They should not put a grade for their notes until you actually put the grade on their notes paper – which you will attempt to do over the next two days.

Task	Title	Date	Notes	Initial
	ADDING INTEGERS STATION			
1	Watch Video 1 and 2	8/25	100%	R.T.
2	Take Notes with Video	8/25		R.T.
3	IXL.com - N.2 Add Integers		70 pts	
4	Add Integers 1 - Worksheet			
5	Add Integers Reteach 1 - Worksheet			
QUIZ 1				

Day 2 and 3

Day 2 and 3 are both independent practice days. Remind students of two expectations prior to beginning the station work. The first is that the students are checking the answer key to make sure that they are getting the problems correct, but they only do so AFTER they've answered the problem. The second expectation is that they consult their notes before asking for help.

As students are doing the independent work, your job is to circulate the room and help students as needed. Try to get to everyone at some point during the class. Don't forget to check their notes as you move throughout the room, either giving them an A+ or writing comments on their paper that explains what they need to add to their notes to get an A+.

Again, if the students finish Task 3 on Day 2 they may move on to Task 4 even if it is not the third day. When they finish Task 4, whether it's on Day 2 or 3, they should immediately move on to Task 5, the extension activity.

At the end of each day, remind students to sign off on their student tracking form, and give themselves a 100% on both Tasks 3 and 4 if they did them correctly and if they checked their answers on the answer keys.

By the end of Day 3, students have completed Task 3 and 4 (the independent practices). They are both due on Day 4, along with the extension activity and their notes. Make sure that all students have their extension activity if they have not started it in class.

Day 4

On Day 4 students take their quiz to see if they have mastered the standard or not.

I do not collect their worksheets and notes until after they have finished the assessment. As you know, it often takes students a while to find all their papers, put them together, and make sure that their name is on it. So I have them do this while they are waiting for everyone else to finish their quizzes, which also affords me more time to grade the papers so that I can do the promotion on Day 4.

After I have finished grading the papers, we play music and I read the names of the students who passed their quiz. They put their name under the banner to memorialize their accomplishment.

If you do not have enough time to celebrate those who passed the quiz, simply do it the next day, which will be Day 1.

After Day 4

The day after Day 4, quiz day, is Day 1 in a new station. If we didn't do the promotions on Day 4, we do it now. Every student has either been promoted to a new station, or they are working on the same station again in a new round.

You do not need to do pre-tests again, that was done initially to determine who was in which station.

Now, every four school days is a rotation, where the students complete the five tasks and take an assessment. So this day is the new Day 1, with everyone on Task 1 and 2, in their new station or in the next round of the same station they just finished but did not pass.

If the student is on a new station, they get a new tracking form. If, however, they are retained on the same station, they use the same tracking form, but work on the next round.

Grading the Round 2 Quiz

If a student completes the station and does not pass the quiz, they must redo the station. When they take the quiz the second time, I like to have the second quiz replace the grade of the first quiz. You, of course, do not have to follow this method, but I like this concept as I want to motivate the kids to succeed, not penalize them for their mistakes.

Chapter 15 – An Overview of What the Day Looks Like

Learning Stations do not replace quality teaching. They are for differentiation, remediation, and acceleration. Learning stations reinforce a skill and help the students master it. But there is much for the teacher to do.

The teacher still must model different concepts, teach vocabulary, dissect word problems, share test-taking strategies, model math thinking, teach new concepts, and a host of other skills that are more practically accomplished in other formats than a learning station.

The learning station, which is dominantly independent practice, should last between 15 – 25 minutes. Which leaves plenty of time to accomplish those other tasks.

Here's what my normal period looks like:

1) Do Now & Whole Group Instruction (10 – 20 minutes)

2) Learning Stations (15 – 25 minutes)

3) Deep Dive – Test Design, Data Chats, Vocabulary, and more (10 – 20 minutes)

Do Now

I teach middle school and high school, so as the students enter the room there are questions on the board that the students must solve. In my class, it is called a 'Do Now,' but you have probably also heard it called a 'Bell Ringer.'

The expectation is that the students will enter the room and go directly to their seat. After getting seated and their supplies out, the students are supposed to immediately begin working on the Do Now questions.

Teacher Tip:

I have the students do their Do Nows on a piece of paper that they hold onto for the entire week. So each day's Do Now is done on this sheet of paper, which I collect on Friday. Doing it this way saves paper, and it saves time with collecting, grading, and passing out papers in class.

Teacher Tip:

I used to have the students do their Do Now problems for the whole week on a blank sheet of paper. The instructions were to number each problem, separate each day's questions by drawing a line across the paper, and to write legibly. As you can imagine, this was a very big ask for the students, and I was constantly getting papers that I could not understand.

So, eventually, I gave in to the frustration and created a standardized Do Now paper for the students so that they knew where to write each problem and show the work, and to make it easy for me to find their answers.

Teacher Tip:

I do not have the students copy the questions of the Do Now if it is a word problem, as this consumes a lot of time – which I would prefer to spend working on math problems or learning. I do, however, require them to copy the equation, as well as the shape or figure if it's a Geometry question. I also require work to be shown.

DO NOW

Copy the problems in the space below, show your work.
Copy the answers in space provided to the right.

1)	2)	3)
4)	5)	6)
7)	8)	9)

1) _____

2) _____

3) _____

4) _____

5) _____

6) _____

7) _____

8) _____

9) _____

This Do Now page is a free download at
www.rethinkmathteacher.com/reach-them-all-downloads

The Do Now usually consists of 4-8 questions (depending on complexity) and are designed to serve at least one of three purposes.

1) Circular Review

2) Test Preparation

3) Introduce a New Skill

I do review the Do Now questions after the time for the students to complete them has ended.

Circular Review

We know that there's a lot covered in a school year and it can be easy to forget some of the learned skills and concepts if they don't stay fresh in the students' minds. So I review key concepts every day during the Do Now to accomplish this task.

At least one Do Now question every day is a question from a previous unit in the curriculum.

Test Preparation

Since the Do Now is done independently by the students, I use the Do Now ˌ opportunity to expose students to questions that will be similar to ˙hat they will see on the end of year diagnostic. This includes ˌnd question that are a deeper depth of knowledge.

ʸ test-taking strategies and model how to think ˌeview the question.

Introduce a New Skill

I also use the Do Now to introduce a new skill to the class. There are usually discovery questions to guide students to an understanding of the new concept – or at least to get them thinking logically about it – in the textbook. I like to have these questions as the last ones on the Do Now, that way we can easily transition into the lesson.

Whole Group Instruction

I typically give my students 4-8 minutes to complete the Do Now questions, depending on their complexity. The students record all the questions and their work on their Do Now paper for the day. During this time, I take attendance and complete any other administrative duties that I need to take care of. I also circulate the room, encouraging students to finish their work and making other observations to help the students do the work correctly.

As previously mentioned, I place a high emphasis on immediate feedback. This allows students to learn from their mistakes, or grow their confidence as they realize that they are doing the questions correctly. So after the allotted time to complete the Do Now, I go over most, or all, of the questions. This also allows me to use each of the questions as a teaching tool and we can talk about best practices and I can give test taking strategies.

After we have finished reviewing the Do Now, we transition into a whole group lesson, and teach a new skill (or continue on the new skill that was introduced in the Do Now). After giving a tutorial on the new skill, and the students have taken notes, we do some practice problems together to review the skill. Then we transition into our learning stations, but we can pick back up on this new skill at the end of class. Of course, we will also work on it again the next day during the Do Now.

The first ten to twenty minutes of class have been dedicated to a Do Now and a Whole Group instruction. During this time, we have done a circular review, we have introduced a new skill and taken notes on it, and we have done some deeper rigor questions with immediate feedback.

> **Teacher Tip:**
>
> One of my favorite teaching strategies is to circulate the room with a marker as students are working on their Do Now. If a student is working as expected, I put a "+10" on their paper, signifying that they have earned 10 points extra credit.
>
> This encourages the students to do their work, and to follow the classroom expectations. I don't have to yell at the students or make reminders, I simply walk around the room with a marker and the students get on task. I also make a point to thank, out loud, the students who are doing a good job as I put the extra credit points on their paper.

A Quick Note

When choosing what skills or standards to do for the whole group instruction, I try to select something that the majority of the class can do or ones that do not have a lot of prerequisite skills attached to them. For example, in sixth grade, I do not like to do circles for the whole group time until all students have mastered multiplying with decimals. The reason is that circles are very difficult for sixth-grade students because they have to memorize the circle formula, they have to correctly apply it to an image, and they have to be able to multiply with decimals. Those are very hard skills that the majority of the class cannot do. So instead of making the whole class work on this, when only half (or less) are going to get much out this time, I tend to focus on skills that everyone in the room can complete, like identifying integers and placing them on a number line. The standard for finding the area and circumference of circles can become a station that students will get to once they have mastered other concepts.

Learning Station Time

After completing the Do Now, we then transition into our learning stations. As we've discussed in this book, the students will be in stations working on different skills, but all students are doing the same thing (a tutorial, a worksheet, etc).

I begin station time by asking students to take out their student tracking paper so that they can see what skill and task they are working on. They also need to take out the notes that they took in Task 2 since they will need to reference them as they do the independent work. I remind students where the laptops are if they're working online, or where the worksheets and answer sheets are if we're doing independent practice. I also review some other logistical items – like using the answer keys after they've completed the question, checking their notes before they ask a teacher for help, and completing the student tracking form at the end of the station time. I also review login information if the students are working online on a website like Khan Academy or IXL.

We also spend a quick minute talking about pacing, so that everyone knows when his or her papers are due, including the extension activity, Task 5.

After spending a few minutes reviewing everything so that we can have a successful and productive station time, the students begin their station work. As the teacher, I begin by making sure everyone gets started and that there are no issues – fixing computer errors, helping students find the appropriate worksheet, etc. After everyone has started working, I then spend the rest of the time visiting students and monitoring their work. I basically turn into a coach; encouraging students to work through difficult problems and helping students discover how to do the work correctly.

If the time is going well, I extend station time, and if it's not going well I will cut it short, but it typically lasts between 15 and 25 minutes. As the time is coming to an end, I give students reminders that we have "five minutes left," "three minutes left," etc.

When station time has come to an end, I have the students clean up and complete their tracking form. I don't collect any papers until the day of the quiz, so the students must hold onto them in their folders with their notes and tracking forms. As soon as everyone has cleaned up, I do remind them about pacing, and when the extension activity is due in case they need to take it home for homework. Also, if students did not complete the independent work in class, they need to do it for homework. They're allowed to finish it the next day in class, but I encourage them to do it as homework instead.

Deep Dive

With the remaining ten to twenty minutes of class, we focus on the end of year assessment. This usually is in the form of data chats and test practice. For example, we might look at a test-like question that we have previously done, and examine how many students got it correct. We then will look at the incorrect answer that the majority of the class selected (called a 'distractor') and discuss why a student would have selected that as the correct answer and what mistake was made. We also review how to get to the correct answer. Finally, we will do a similar question and review.

Another strategy that's good for this part of class is vocabulary review. For example, in seventh grade, much of the curriculum is related to ratios. So we might review the terms 'ratio,' 'rate,' 'unit rate,' 'percent,' and 'constant rate of change.'

Besides these words, we look at terms that the students might see in the word problems associated with this concept. For example, when dealing with 'percent increase or decrease,' the word problems often revolve around putting money in or out of a bank account. However, most seventh grade students have never used a bank account, and are unfamiliar with the terms 'withdrawal' and 'deposit.' So we review those words. We also talk about 'sales tax' and 'discount' as these are also words that commonly appear in the word problems that students often don't understand.

Finally, we often look at test design. We talk about multiple choice versus multiple select. We look at drag and drop style questions and how to complete them. We will also talk about the best strategies for the other question formats, such as graphing and filling in the blank. The districts and states usually provide practice tests online, which are good opportunities to look at the formatting of the test. This way, when students take the assessment, they are less likely to experience testing anxiety because they're familiar with the design.

Conclusion

I included this chapter because so many people have had questions about what a normal class day looks like when using learning stations. Hopefully, this brief walk-through has given you a good idea of how the days look. For more questions about Learning Stations, go to chapter 15.

Chapter 16 – Frequently Asked Questions

Now that you know what the station rotations look like and how to implement it in your classroom, we need to discuss other frequently asked questions about implementation.

How long does station work last?

The station length will be different for everyone, depending on the classroom setup, age and maturity of the students, and a few other factors. But I find that they typically last between 15 and 25 minutes, depending on how everything is going. Some days the students are working hard, and everything's going well, and it lasts longer than normal. And some days, the opposite is true.

Of course, some of this time is students getting laptops and headphones, or the textbooks and worksheets, as well as checking answer sheets and completing the tracking form which may add a few minutes to your timeline, but generally speaking, 15-25 minutes is accurate and sufficient.

Do you do station work every day?

Yes. Every day, with obvious exceptions for school functions, testing, etc.

I just keep rotating through the four days of work.

Is the station work done the entire period?

No, the students only work in the station for a section of the class, typically 15-25 minutes.

Remember that it's hard for anyone, regardless of age, to do one thing for an entire 50 minutes (or however long your class period is). So stations lend very well to chunking.

What does the rest of the day look like?

I begin class with a Do Now. So that as students enter the room, they immediately begin working on math. While they are completing the Do Now, this also allows me to take roll and complete other tasks that I am expected to do as the teacher.

The first task, the Do Now, consists of a few questions on the board that the students answer independently on paper and then we review together. This often transitions into a brief period of whole group instruction.

I try to use this time to teach or review a standard that the students can all do. So it's either something that we have already mastered or on a standard that doesn't have that many prerequisite skills.

This work normally is 10-20 minutes.

After station work, I like to do test preparation work. So sometimes we look at test design – which is looking at the type of questions you will see on the end of year diagnostic (like drag and drop, multiple select, fill in the blank, graphing, etc.). We will often spend time looking at data from previous assessments and discuss common errors we are making and why we are making them.

The end of class time is also where we will work on word problems, though we also do these a lot in the Do Now as well. It is important to spend time each day focusing on word problems, which are usually deeper rigor, so that the students get sufficient practice on them before the diagnostic.

To conclude, we begin class with a Do Now and some instruction, we transition to station work, and we end with test prep or data analysis.

But I have to follow the pacing guide

Many teachers tell me that they are required to teach certain standards on certain days or that they must follow the pacing guide given to them by their school or district.

Learning station should not get in the way of this. Remember that the learning station is just 15-25 minutes of class time, so you can use the other time to teach the material that is supposed to be taught by the pacing guide that you are following.

The stations are your remediation or your acceleration. And since you are collecting data every four days, all you have to do is align this data to the standards and your administrators will be very satisfied with what you are doing.

What do you do when someone is absent?

If a student misses the pre-test day, they take it on the day that they return. The teacher must grade it on the spot, and then put the student in a station immediately so that the student can get into the station work.

Any other time a student is absent, they are put into their rotation and must work through the work. They'll have to complete at least one of the tasks at home for homework because you want them to take the quiz on Day 4 with the rest of the class, or keeping track of where everyone is will become difficult for you, the teacher.

It's important that the student has the opportunity complete the tutorial and the notes before doing the independent work, so if a student misses Day 1, I have them do Task 1 and 2 on the day that they return.

However, if the student misses day 2 or 3, they have to complete tasks 3 and 4 either in class or for homework; all work is due on day 4. (I normally wave the extension activity if the student was absent, and I indicate this on his student tracking form which I sign.)

If the student misses multiple days in the four-day rotation they are still responsible for making up the first 4 tasks (or all 5 if you like) and taking the quiz on Day 4. Obviously, if they were only in class for one of the three days, they most likely will not pass the quiz. But this is why I like having the grade of the quiz of the second round replace the grade of the quiz on the first round if the student repeats the station.

How do you grade their work?

This is one of the questions that I am most often asked when I am teaching about learning stations. Most teachers ask because they are required to give a certain amount of grades per week or per quarter.

However, grading student work the way that we have been discussing is actually not difficult at all.

Every four days, each student has completed five tasks, each of which can be graded, though I normally don't give a grade for watching the videos. Remember tasks 3 and 4, the independent practices, have instant feedback. So the students should have 100% on both of them. All you really should have to do is check for completion. (I know that this is not always the case, so I do spot check the papers from time to time). So you should be able to get at least five grades in the book from these three days of work, plus a quiz. Not to mention that you can be doing other assignments during the rest of the class period.

One quick note, most of the grades I give are just completion grades since the answer sheets are provided.

Do You Build a Station for Each Skill in the Curriculum?

I do not. Of course, you are welcome to, but that is a lot of work. I take several of the more dominant standards in the curriculum – and typically, the ones that have more prerequisite skills in them – and build stations for them. Other standards are taught during the other parts of class that we discussed in Chapter 15.

For example, when I taught Pre-Algebra, I looked at the standards and noticed that if I taught all the skills Solving Systems of Equations by Graphing, I would cover a large chunk of the standards. For example, one of the prerequisite skills for this would be slope, which is a Pre-Algebra standard. As is graphing a line, which you must learn to be able to graph two lines and determine where they intersect. So I built four or five stations for this one standard, as well as four or five for Two-Step Equations, and that covered a large part of the standards for the year. Other skills were taught during the Do Now and whole group instruction time, and most of those skills didn't need all the prerequisite stations to master.

How Many Stations Should I Create to Start?

I would recommend starting with one skill, that is a bit more involved, and more important in terms of weight on the end of year diagnostic. Build your prerequisite stations for that one skill, and go from there. It's okay if you only have a few, that's a great place to start. Don't feel pressured to build one for every standard in the class, nor to have a bunch in place to get started. If you only have one, that's okay, start there and build as you go.

Aren't You Just Teaching to the Test?

For a few years I taught sixth-grade Social Studies at a small private school. At the end of the year, they gave the students the Iowa Test of Basic Skills, to see how we compared with students around the country.

The problem was that our sixth-grade curriculum was World History, and the test was on American History. So our scores didn't look good, because they were being tested on something they hadn't been taught. We weren't teaching to the test.

The above question always bothers me, because before the state got involved with all of these diagnostics, teachers still gave tests, and they still used that information to measure proficiency. And what kind of teacher would test you on something you hadn't been learning?

So yes, I am preparing my students to take and master the test, and that is one of my goals for them. And having students truly master some of the curriculum will yield much higher scores on that test then pushing them through the entire curriculum without them mastering any of it.

But beyond that, I am focusing on growth. In the classroom I have outlined in this book, mastery is expected and celebrated. Students are free to wrestle and struggle with material without being punished or left behind or marginalized. This success does show itself on the state diagnostic, but it also shows in the student's sentiments towards school and math, as well as in classroom management.

They won't Get Through the Entire Curriculum in the Year

Think about the students that entered your room this year. How many of them do you think mastered the entire curriculum last year? How many of them were exposed to much of the curriculum, but mastered little of it?

Would you rather your students see all of the curriculum, but comprehend none of it, or see some of the curriculum, but master all of what they were exposed to.

There is no value in showing students math concepts if they don't understand it. Let them go at the pace that they need to move at and trust the process. Again, they will grow, and that should be the goal.

What if I Teach a Block Scheduling

Obviously, there are different variations of block scheduling. But the main premise that you have them your class for two periods in a row, and then you will not have them for two periods in a row, instead of one period every day.

I have been teaching you to chunk the six tasks into four days, and to complete one day each period. So if you are using a block schedule, I would recommend to complete two days' worth of tasks in one block.

For example, if you have your students for two periods on Monday and Wednesday, I suggest doing Day 1 and Day 2 on Monday (which is Task 1 through Task 3) and Day 3 and Day 4 on Wednesday (which is Task 4 through 6).

In this scenario, I would recommend making the extension activity the homework between the two days that you have your students, but that might not be ideal for you. In which case, you would adjust accordingly.

I do not recommend, however, that you do the Day 1 and Day 2 task consecutively. In other words, I would have them do their station time for the allotted 15-25 minutes, then do some other activity, then come back to another 15-25 minute station activity later in the block. This is because it is hard for anyone, especially a young student, to stay focused on one thing for 30 – 50 minutes in a row. Chunking up the period will yield better results in most circumstances.

What if the Student Passes Every Section on the Pre-Test?

If the student gets a 100% on the pre-test, then they have no station to go to, since each section of the pre-test corresponded with one station and they just tested out of all of the stations. In this scenario, they should be given the next pre-test for the next set of stations to see what they need to work on.

That said, when you are just beginning, you may not have the next group of stations ready to go, so you will have to get creative. I have done many things in this scenario. I have made that student a coach and assigned her to work with other students, helping them on their station work. I have made that student a teacher, and given them the responsibility of preparing the next lesson and teaching it. I have also given these students the challenge of creating their own learning station. Finally, in some circumstances, I have put the textbook in front of the student, turned to the next section, and treated that like the student's station work. So I have opened to the next unit, told the student to read the tutorial and take notes. Then I have assigned the student practice problems and given them an answer key to check their work.

All of the above options can work, and you should pick the one that you think will work best for you (or something else that I have not mentioned above).

Conclusion

I hope that you are excited about reaching your students. This method truly does work, and your students will love it. You will see a noticeable difference in your classroom, both in the way they act, and how they approach their education.

If you haven't done so already, look at your upcoming lesson. What skill will the students be working on? What prerequisite skills should they already know to master that skill? Write those down, build a station for each, and start plugging your students into those stations so that they can truly master the skill.

Thank you for reading.

Sincerely,

Chris Skierski

Chris Skierski
RethinkMathTeacher.com

Bibliography

Khan, Sal. "Let's Use Video to Reinvent Education." TED. Mar. 2011. Lecture.

https://www.ted.com/talks/salman_khan_let_s_use_video_to_reinvent_education

93240565R00066

Made in the USA
San Bernardino, CA
07 November 2018